Casino Con

An Eye-Opening Look from the Inside Out

Part I – The Ruse

By
E.A. James

FM Publishing Company
Cherokee, NC 28719

Casino Con

An Eye-Opening Look from the Inside Out
Part I – The Ruse

ISBN 9781931671507

Library of Congress Control Number 2013951292

Copyright © 2013 by Elizabeth Abigail James

FM Publishing Company

P.O. Box 215

Cherokee, NC 28719

FM Publishing Co.

Dedication

This book is dedicated to every hardworking, stressed out, underpaid, overworked, and dehumanized non-management black employee in the casino industry. It is dedicated to all of those who have been negatively affected because of favoritism, racism, and discrimination, and to those who have, for years, felt helpless to do anything about it. It is also dedicated to those who have yet to understand that slavery is one of the most awful institutions created and sanctioned by the government, and that (contrary to popular belief) it is still with us today but has merely taken on different forms. May God bless you and be with you as you move forward in His love and Spirit, remembering to keep your head up and allow his precious light to shine upon you.

Preface

This book is non-fiction and is based on real events, situations, conversations, reflections, and experiences. They are told in chronological order and occur over a period of about two years, not including past reflections. Please note that specific company confidential information and dates of the year have been eliminated. In addition, the 140 names of individuals have been changed to protect the innocent against the guilty.

The foregoing pages represent the first part of a three-part series called Casino Con, Part I – The Ruse. The Ruse presents the lies and deception to which we, as black people, have become accustomed; however, when truth is revealed, there should be a change in mindset to move forward and to make sure *you* are no longer a part of the deception but become the exception.

Table of Contents

Table of Contents (cont'd)

Introduction

How We Got There

Little did my daughter and I realize that the coming next year would teach us a lesson about gambling and the casino life that we would never forget. People like us have had so many disappointments and setbacks in life because we are descendants of slaves who also became the victims of Jim Crow laws, and continual and ongoing racism, bigotry, and discrimination. It never stops; it's like a chameleon. It just disguises itself, changes forms, and keeps right on oppressing its victims. It also reminds me of the AIDs virus' T-Cell. It is so deceptive and so deadly. It infiltrates without being noticed because the rest of the body is naïve, unsuspecting, and seemingly immune. It reveals itself and attacks the immune system before the body knows what's happening. The T-Cell (I call it the Takeover Cell) has already begun its work. It's already had time to do irreparable damage. As technology increases and improves, scientists and doctors have found ways to minimize some of the dangerous effects (constitutional amendments, civil rights laws, affirmative action). However, for a healthy body, true "reparations" have not been achieved.

So, we try to find quick fixes by buying scratchers and playing the lottery every week. We spend what little hard-earned money we have in search of getting rich or at least getting enough money to get the creditors off our backs and hopefully buy a few finer things in life. We envy those few who have been allowed in the "big house." These are those who, among the millions who are smart and talented and can run, sing, act, dance, and can do amazing things with a ball in sports, have been set apart and noticed. They have been allowed to enjoy some of the seemingly sweet fruits of the good life. They make a lot of money, but they also spend a lot of money – usually they just give it back to the same people who gave it to them. They have been bought with a price, usually 30 pieces of silver, where the real cost is the lives of the entire race of people. We are so unaware of the true evil that has been done. We have been "white-washed," brain-washed, and made to love our oppressors. The devil is our true oppressor. He tricks us and holds out carrots just beyond our reach. He makes us believe that the carrots are the best thing since water and that we are virtually nothing or nobody without them. He does this to us continually. Each carrot achieved leads to another and another. None of them are satisfying because we are so ignorant and deceived we do not realize that the carrots are superficial and fake. They are not satisfying because they were never intended to be.

Gambling and the casino experience is only one type of deception. Sometimes it involves others such as drugs, alcoholism, illicit sex, pornography, homosexuality, gluttony, and the quest for material goods. They lead to a life that is spiritually empty and hollow, despite what others think or feel. Many will take offense to the inclusion of homosexuality because of the popular beliefs, but God is not interested in what is popular, only what is true and righteous. We all have to ultimately answer to him and not to each other. Man's physical existence is but a breath that fades and like the green grass that withers away. How we live the life we've been given here for this short sojourn is in what God is concerned. Jesus said that not everyone who calls him "Lord, Lord" will enter into His Father's kingdom, but those who "do the will of my Father in Heaven."

So, after countless employment doors closing, the one that opened was at the casino, the very place we had been spending a great amount of time, the very place that had taken lots of our hard-earned dollars, and the very place that would be the beginning of a very hard lesson. It would also be the seed of an even higher objective and goal that the Father wanted us to achieve. Herein is one former gambler's and consequently one former gaming employee's story.

Chapter 1

Gambling and Rambling

March 4 – Because of my wonderful talent for losing money at the casino, I achieved Platinum status. Not only did I come in and get a nice new shiny blue/gray Total Rewards card, but I had received (via email) an invitation for 2-4 nights of complimentary stay at the Harrah's Cherokee Casino & Resort. Their hotel was beautiful and much more comfortable than sleeping on those air bags we owned. They had a few channels of free movies, we could order room service and pay with our rewards credits, and we had a nice place to sleep in between playing the slots, gambling at the tables (Black Jack, 3-Card Poker, Pai-Gow), and playing poker. We had been there about 5-6 times. Any winnings, which were minimal, were always short-lived. My daughter did not play slots, but the end result was always the same no matter what each of us played.

It is an addictive habit because it is designed to be so. It does not matter how much literature and wall postings they put up that talks about their policy with regard to Responsible Gaming. It does not matter how much money a person gambles, it is all relative. What may seem like a lot to one person, because of his or her income level, may seem like a small amount to someone else whose income level is much higher. The experience is all the same. The goal is to bleed you slowly while making you believe you're having a great time. You're left anemic and near death with a smile on your face.

I used to wonder why so many ministers used to preach against gambling. I couldn't understand it. I thought it was just like anything else. It's entertainment on which you spend your money. It's just another way of having fun, and like everything else, you have to pay for it. I would soon learn, from looking at it from the inside out, how wrong I was. No one makes people gamble; this is true. However, no one tells them the real and complete truth either, and this book is designed to do just that.

Chapter 2

High Expectations

March 18 – My daughter and I were hired. She was offered the interview for the Cage Cashier while I was offered the Total Rewards Representative position. Below is a copy of the Total Rewards Representative job description:

> Enter new customer accounts into the database, verify existing accounts and ensure database accuracy; assist in the execution of floor promotions and special events as needed; greet customers as a company representative and provide information concerning casino programs and amenities, off-site attractions, hotels and restaurants, and Harrah's Total Reward program; issue promotional amenities, redeem coupons, and maintain accurate banks and inventory control records; complete reports, schedule and facilitate arrival/departure of motor coaches; resolve customer incidents and issues as they arise; participate on task forces, special projects, and committees

> Greet motor coaches, accurately distributing proper incentives to motor coaches, and distribute Total Rewards Program to players across the casino floor by advertising the benefits

> Delight our guests with outstanding resort level service

> Proactive with incidents and issues ensuring resolution with employees and guests

> Be a participative member of the team by volunteering and being involved in buzz sessions, projects, committees, and task forces by providing input and suggestions

> Other duties as requested to deliver excellent service to internal and external customers

> > ➤ Maintain a clean and orderly work environment
> > ➤ Maintain environment of readiness pertaining to supplies, resources, and tools to perform job duties

> ➤ Adhere to regulatory, departmental and company polices in an ethical manner

Both my daughter and I went through New Hire Training with Helen; my daughter and I went through the training at the same time since we were hired the same day. I passed all of my preliminaries and exams. In addition, I was told by my peers what a great job I did during our first spotlight when judged by 3 other HR Personnel. Helen told us to just show up for work every day and that as long as we were upbeat and positive with the guests, they would be forgiving even if we made mistakes. I noticed that the only Black person I saw was a woman who worked in HR. I would only see her one time thereafter. She had a short natural, wore street clothes (pants and a top), and told us not to drink out of the cups in the EDR and to get plenty of Airborne. She said the Airborne would help keep us healthy. We would later discover that she was right. It would take some time to get used to the environment – germs and smoke.

My daughter received full-time status after the first two weeks. I would learn later that most of them assumed she was an enrolled member because of the way she looked. However, once they discovered this was not the case, her casino employment would, like mine, take an entirely different turn.

Chapter 3

First Time for Everything

March – I received a letter from Mendleson, the supposedly "big wig" at Harrah's Cherokee, inviting me to take advantage of all the great promotion and advancement opportunities available at the exciting and wonderful Harrah's Cherokee Casino & Resort.

I was not assigned a supervisor because I believe they were in transition. Although I was the only one hired in TR during the week of March 18th, I discovered that others had been hired 2 weeks prior and subsequently, 2 weeks after me; others a month to 2 months after me. I was trained by Victoria who had just gotten back from burying her mother. She was not UPA and understandably so. She had been gone, so she was not aware of some of the new procedures but tried to familiarize herself with them. I enjoyed working at the Earth Water TR's area because it was non-smoking and not as noisy; however, I noticed that Ethel would only assign me upstairs a few times. While up there, I would shadow Alma, a former Black female co-worker. She shared with me that when she was hired she told Ethel that she was going to transfer to Table Games after her 90 days. She was already an experienced dealer. Alma was friendly and very proficient at her job, so I learned as much from her as I could. I enjoyed working with the rest of the staff also. Everything was new, but I caught on very quickly. When clean-up time came, I started cleaning all the way down at the farthest end; however, I was told by a co-worker that they only clean or replace embosser reels from the middle stations up to the 7-Star station. I thought this odd because dust collects even when stations are not used. I had a $10 coupon missing. Here's a copy of the letter to Ethel:

    Date: Friday, March 29

To: Ethel, Total Rewards Supervisor

From: Rachel, Total Rewards Representative
Re: $10 Variance on Thursday, March 28

When told that I was short one of the $10 redeemable for cash vouchers on Thursday, March 28th, I was not only surprised but disturbed as well. Although we are all human and make mistakes, I tried my best to be extremely careful and to make sure I gave out (as needed and appropriate) only one of the $5, $10, and $20 vouchers that I was issued.

Something happened earlier that day that was a bit daunting but it didn't really dawn on me until the ride home when I was racking my brain to try and figure out how I could have "lost" one of the $10 coupons. I remember Teresa telling me a few minutes after I'd gotten back from my last 15-minute break that she noticed that I set my money pack back on the counter and then left for a moment to go get a drink in the office. I did do this but I remember that we weren't busy during this time. However, she told me that I need to make sure that I set my money pack in my chair so none of the guests could just reach over and grab anything. I thanked her and told her she was absolutely right and that I hadn't thought of that. However, I don't believe this is when it might have happened. Earlier that day, the only other time I believe it could have happened was when I was using the terminal at the farther end. I had given out a $60 groupon and a $30 groupon, but because we were busy, I don't believe I put the paper clip back on; in fact, I remember dropping the paper clip on the floor and bending down to retrieve it. Also, I remember leaving my station to get Felicia to show me how to put a picture on a Seven Star member's card. This was the longest time I was away, but I'm not sure if it happened then or not. The oddest thing I remember that day is that at one point I noticed my group of $5 coupons, along with my voided tickets, on the floor. I remember thinking how strange this was but it didn't really register at the time. It was odd because I know that I'm usually aware at the time if something drops on the floor. In retrospect, it's possible someone could have taken one of the $10 coupons when it was loose and because I know I had my $5 coupons and tickets on top, they knocked these on the floor when taking it.

Please know that this is only what I believe may have happened and when. I don't want to unduly accuse anyone of anything. If it is at all possible to run back the surveillance tape to check this, I would greatly appreciate it. I know that I am responsible for my issued coupons (money) and must be more careful. I believe I was just a little too trusting. It's disappointing when I think that one of those guests just smiled at me all the while taking the $10. It seems such an insignificant amount, but I've been told by other reps that some of the guests will lie for a few dollars. Also, I want to make sure that just because my daughter works as a cage cashier and that we were in need of monetary resources a few days prior to this that no one thinks we were in cahoots or something. Aside from the fact, that no matter what, my daughter and I would never resort to this type of thing because we always rely on God to supply all of our needs, please know that on Wednesday, March 27th my daughter and I received a check from The C.A.R.E. Fund to help us with our move transition and other resources. We cashed this check earlier on Thursday, March 28th before we came to work. So, at that time we were no longer in need of anything.

Please accept my apologies that I allowed this variance to occur. My goal is to make sure I keep better tabs on my money pack and its contents. Thank you and I appreciate your help and support.

Sincerely,

Rachel
Total Rewards Representative

I would discover later that this little display of initiative, assertiveness, and intelligence would be the catalyst that started my career toward the road of "no return on investment."

Chapter 4

Get the Point?

April – The job seemed to be going well. Hours got longer and I was sent to the Rotunda TR most of the time. Several co-workers came in sick with the flu. Apparently they were contagious. I got really sick and on a Saturday, I was throwing up and had diarrhea at the same time. I was still fairly new. We received a lot of information during the New Employee Orientation, so I did not remember everything. Also, since I was ill, my mental acuity was not up to par. I called the TR Dept. to let them know I was not feeling well and would not be in. Natasha answered the phone and told me that I needed to call the Blind Man's Bluff and gave me the extension. She said this department would call TR to let them know I would not be in. So, I did this, not realizing I would receive 3 points on my attendance because it was a weekend. It would have been nice if someone had advised me at that time (reminded me) of this and/or told me that I could have used an emergency day or possibly drag myself in and be sent home on EO. This would have helped me greatly. However, I don't fault them for this; this was my responsibility.

I learned to do Combines when there were duplicate accounts. I learned this from Natasha and Linda. It was fairly easy once I understood the process. Linda was able to explain it a little better than Natasha. When I told Ethel that I knew how to do Combines, she told me that I shouldn't ask her anything about them because she didn't know how to do them. I thought this was odd because she was a supervisor. However, I didn't say anything to her about it. I was told by Eunice that she was concerned because the new people were learning how to do Combines and that she didn't have an opportunity to learn them.

I sent a letter to Ivan, TR Manager, dated April 12 because I saw such inconsistencies in the department that greatly

17

disturbed me. I am a Certified Manager of Program Improvement, and it is in me to offer suggestions and try to find a way to restore balance. However, I would realize later that this would come back to "bite" me. I saw Ivan in the hallway when coming into work one evening and briefly talked with him. He explained that everyone (supervisors) did everything right but he would talk with them about being consistent. He told me that the new staff usually get the "crappy hours." He also said that as new people are hired, more options would open up. He also told me that they could not have a procedures manual because it would be 2 inches thick and would be constantly changing. I did not agree but did not tell him so. I felt that a manual for the CRM was pretty constant.

I was told not to be too disturbed by write-ups because everybody gets them. I noticed that Ethel was sending me to Rotunda most of the time, so I decided to make it easier and told her I like going to the Rotunda. This way she didn't have to make a decision.

Because of a special promotion, I, along with the other TR's, was responsible for close to $15,000 worth of coupons – each day for three consecutive days. I hand counted coupons at the beginning and end of the shift on days 2 and 3 and hand counted coupons at end of shift only on day 1. I had zero-variance for all three days. For someone who had only been there for less than 90 days, this should have been something praiseworthy; however, this did not happen. I would learn later that others (not my skin color and race) would receive praise for accomplishing much less.

Chapter 5

Full-Time Hours, Part-Time Jobs

May – I could tell my blood pressure was high because my head hurt and I wasn't feeling well. I told Natasha not to panic but that I needed to have an EMT check my blood pressure during my break. She called them over. My blood pressure was very high; however, I was still functioning well. I decided to go home early to take care of my health.

I overheard a co-worker stating that Beverly was going to receive a full-time position. I had previously asked my co-worker and trainer, Victoria, if we were supposed to formally request a full-time position. She told me "No, they would come to you." Therefore, the fact that I heard that a co-worker hired after me was being offered full-time bothered me a little. Felicia asked me if I was interested in a full-time position, and I told her that if they were going to work me full-time, then I should be full-time. I was trying to be content in a part-time position; however, I later discovered that I would need benefits, especially medical, by the beginning of the next year. Also, I was no longer working an extra part-time position online (10 hours per week) and I didn't learn how Cherokee's structure worked until later. I thought that a part-time position was always a part-time position and I also learned that full-time staff had priority over part-time staff when it came to lay-offs. I wanted to keep my seniority, if possible.

 Felicia, who later became my supervisor, called me in and had me check "Yes" or "No" on a sheet if I would be willing to take a full-time position; however, she indicated that the only hours available were 11pm to 7:30am. I checked "Yes" that I would be interested. She then told me that there were several others who were hired before me (seniority) who would have first choice if they were interested.

I ended up sitting in the 7-Star chair for several hours at the Rotunda next to Lance, a co-worker. He later told me that he was "very impressed." He said that it took him 5 months before he could "learn all of that stuff." He told me it was a pleasure sitting next to me. I thanked him for saying so. Lance also brought down to the Rotunda a Combine for duplicate accounts because he said he wanted to get the process down. I showed him the step that he was missing.

I showed Barbara how to do Combines; she was really sharp and caught on immediately. However, Muriel told me to just let her get her "feet wet" first. However, Barbara did finish one of the Combines and told me that they were easier than everything else.

I've been noticing that quite a lot of the accounts were missing phone numbers, email addresses, and license information, especially "00" where the expiration dates should be. When a guest's account information is verified, I noticed that a lot of the TR reps would hit the F12 screen to take them into the guest account. Although they would then hit "F1" and then proceed to print a card for the guest, they would not go back into the "41" screen and then update the guest's license information, especially if the guest confirmed that the address was correct. I tried to tell this to two of the D/R supervisors at the Earth Water, but they just said everyone should be checking that the information is correct. It was an oversight that new reps would make, but I don't believe they truly understood what I was talking about, so I just made a point to make the changes myself.

I had another $5 variance (coupon). I received a write-up for re-writing a coupon for "Host Cash." I would discover later, much to my dismay, that this was given a Code 10 which was very serious; however, it would take me at least 5 months later to make this discovery. I made a point not to repeat this error. I received a write-up for forgetting to stamp one of the $5 coupon receipts "VOID." I noted that the supervisor who counted me out had also not caught this before submitting to Internal Control. I made a point not to repeat this error.

Chapter 6

Write-Up, Up and Away!

I still noticed inconsistencies in the department. I noticed that Beverly would go to break and leave her coupon bag in the crevice of her chair when she was in the Diamond chair because she wanted to make sure she would sit there when she returned. When she did this again at the Rotunda, I mentioned this to Muriel to remind Beverly to lock up her bag. I noticed that on one occasion, Beverly had stamped a RC redemption sheet "VOID" that was not supposed to be stamped because the guest was going to take it to the cashier. She went to Natasha with whom she has a good rapport because they are both of Mexican-descent and speak Spanish with each other when conversing. This was a mistake that impacted a guest and not just a matter of procedures for Internal Control. However, I am certain Beverly did not receive a write-up for this. My belief is that Natasha found a way to correct the problem. I only bring this up because every little mistake is usually given a write-up and used as training tools and does not allow very much for human error. Even so, there should be consistency.

I received a write-up for re-writing a coupon for a Diamond-player who apparently had already had the coupon re-written for him. I submitted a verbal argument to my supervisor that it was not my error but the fault was with the guest. However, I was told that Edward, one of the other supervisors, insisted that it was my job to read all of the guest comments and see that the coupon had already been re-written. I initialed the write-up by putting on there that I refused to sign in protest. I did not make any comments but my refusal to sign was for the following reasons: (1) The coupon was still valid and had not been redeemed when I re-wrote it for the guest; (2) From the copy of the receipts, it is clearly seen that the food credit coupon re-written by another co-worker was redeemed later that same day AFTER I re-wrote the food credit coupon, and the coupon that I re-wrote was redeemed the very next day. Since this was done at the Food Court and the staff do not have access to the CRM system (I assume), there was no way of knowing the guest was redeeming the same coupon twice. Therefore, I became the "fall person." Either the guest was pulling a fast one or the guest was unaware that it was for the same coupon; (3) Even if I had noticed that the coupon had been re-written by another rep, the guest told me he did not have it. Since it showed that it had not been redeemed (it was still in green in the system, not pink), my job was to re-write coupons for 7-Stars, Diamonds, and guests with a representative. So this is what I did. I felt a write-up was unjustified because I was written up for simply doing what I was supposed to do.

I received a top-box internal spotlight from Muriel. Our work rapport had greatly improved. She told me that she did not have to worry about me because I always started cleaning the embossers and the area without being told to do so.

I noticed that I was being watched on several occasions by outside staff and a few times by the Tribal Gaming Commission. I knew this because when the individual left, Zelda told me who the person was; however, I never received any feedback. I was being told by guests what a great service I had given them, but my supervisors never received any feedback. I noticed that several co-workers received written compliments about the service they had provided to guests.

A co-worker, Morris, who later became Manager of the Diamond Lounge, was leaving and I mentioned to Victoria that I wanted to get a card for him so everyone can sign. She ended up buying one in the EDR and we all signed it. I mention items like this because I always try to show others they are appreciated, no matter who they are.

May 18 – I submitted a memo to Felicia regarding my work hours:

I've only been here 60 days, so I'm unaware if there is a form to complete for this request, and therefore, am submitting it to you in this format.

Is it possible to ask Jack, the TR Supervisor who does the work schedule, to schedule me with hours that will not leave me with burnout? For example, I come in on Fridays from 8pm to 4:30am and then back to work within 12 hours on Saturday at 5pm. The 5pm to 1:30 am is great; however, it's the quick turnaround the day before that leaves me tired, drained, and not rested. This could greatly impact my ability to be an effective TR representative and "top box" with guests. I know that I have seniority over Zelda, Barbara, and Beverly because I was hired before them. Is it possible to change my schedule with the days and hours that Jack is giving to Barbara or Beverly? I am formally requesting this at the present time.

I worked in Personnel for 6 years and have been an office manager and director over several programs, so I do understand a little about employee burnout. I love working here with my co-workers, staff, and guests, and want to avoid burnout.

I hope you and Jack sincerely consider my request. Thank you for being the type of supervisor that has invited me to come to you when I have questions and concerns. I greatly appreciate it.

Chapter 7
Competitive Chairs as Carrots

June – I was told by Ethel and Natasha that they always go by seniority (person who has been in TR the longest) when it comes to placing frontline reps in the Seven Star and Diamond chairs. This is because they want the most experienced person providing service to these guests. This applies, I was told, according to those who were on shift in that specific location. However, I noticed this did not apply when it came to Beverly and Barbara, both TR reps who were hired after me.

I received another top-box spotlight from my supervisor, Felicia. However, I noticed that she was a bit confused on a couple of points. It was probably due to her having done a spotlight on more than one rep at a time. She put on the form that I told the guest about the music series that was going on and that I needed to speak louder when we were real busy because it gets noisy. I never recommend the music series to guests; I always recommend that they check out Brio's Italian Tuscan Grille on the 2nd Floor. I do this because I've eaten there many times and love the food.

One of my co-workers, Leslie, appeared perturbed because I was kidding a guest who asked if he needed to put out his cigarette before he came to our window. I told the guest he did if he came to me. Leslie told him he could smoke anywhere he wanted, so he went to her. Leslie has appeared to want to find fault with anything I say or do, but I usually just ignored it. I saw her go to Natasha and Felicia. I later discovered what she told them. I had a female guest who had a cigarette in her hand and came to my station. I asked her if she would blow the smoke in the other direction. The guest just took it upon herself to go and put her cigarette out. Felicia came up behind me and told me not to tell the guests to put out their cigarettes. The guest told her that I didn't say that to her. After the guest left, I asked Felicia if I could speak with her. I told her about the situation and that I was getting tired of Leslie doing things like this. It creates confusion and division. She told me that Leslie would be going to an earlier shift and would not be there anyway. I later heard from one of the co-workers that Leslie told several people that I don't like her. I prayed about this situation and how best to handle it. When I learned that it had been Leslie's birthday and that she was out for a few days, I took it upon myself to get a belated birthday card for her and a congratulations card for Linda who had been promoted to Dual Rate Supervisor. I signed the card and put exactly the same quote on them: "Who can find a virtuous woman, for her price is far above rubies? She opens her mouth with wisdom and in her tongue is the law of kindness." Proverbs 31: 10, 26. It applied to both of them in different ways: Linda exemplified the quote, while Leslie needed to aspire to it.

I came down to the Rotunda one day and one of the reps who had been sitting in the 7-Star chair was leaving, so I sat in either the Diamond or 7-Star chair. Esmerelda, one of my co-workers seemed real perturbed so see me in the chair. A couple came to my station and wanted reward cards. I asked Esmerelda if she would wait on the husband and she complied. While viewing the wife's license, I discovered it had expired and told her I could not create an account for her. I asked Esmerelda if she would print two cards for the husband. She seemed real perturbed and asked me why. I told her so that he would have two cards, which is what I usually do for new card holders, that is, I ask them if they want 1 or 2 cards in case one stops working. Esmerelda knew that the husband would probably let the wife play on his card. However, they were an older couple and did not look under 30. I notice that a lot of the guests play slots on each other's cards. I noticed this when I was a guest, not just an employee. I asked Natasha if she and Esmerelda and I could talk just so there would be no misunderstanding and tension between

Esmerelda and me. We talked it out. Natasha said that we both did something wrong that we hadn't thought about. I apologized to Esmerelda; however, it was not until a few days later when she came down to the Rotunda that she apologized and asked if I was upset. I told her I had already forgotten all about it. All was well.

Chapter 8

Move On Up?

June 18 – My daughter and I applied online for positions. I applied for VIP Host and my daughter applied for Gaming Host. HR called my daughter to advise her that there was a different application procedure for internal applicants. Since my daughter and I live together and I answered the phone, I asked the HR rep about the VIP Host position. She told me to call Olga in HR. I did so and was told that they were looking at an "01" for the position, but if I wanted to apply I needed to do so before Thursday at 4 pm. I went to HR on Wednesday and received a listing but it did not have VIP Host listed. I saw Sr. Account Executive Host and assumed it to be the same position. I thought maybe the title was changed for some reason. Neither Felicia nor Ethel was available, so I went to Edward to get the supervisor signature. He called to find out my points (2) and asked if I'd taken Superlap. I told him they said I had to be there 6 months before I could. He walked me to Ivan's office on the 3rd Floor. Ivan read it over and he and Edward briefly discussed the fact there was no 90-day evaluation. Edward said that HR needed to know what it was but they didn't have to see it. Ivan signed off on it and I turned it in with my resume. I brought my degree transcript the next day.

Thursday, June 20 – While signing in for work in TR, a staff member came in to talk briefly with Ethel. I happen to notice that his badge said Sr. Account Executive Host. I realized that there was no way they could have changed their badges over that quickly, so I must have been mistaken to assume that the VIP Host position title had been changed. I realized then that they were not the same position. I asked one of my co-workers and was told that it was not the same position. I called Helen in HR to ask about it. She said there was an external list and there was an internal list. She said the lady in HR assumed I wanted the internal list since I was already an employee. I called over to Olga and told her I wanted to apply for the VIP Host position. She said she would change the transfer sheet title and send my information over. I never heard back after this.

I heard from several co-workers that Esmerelda had gotten fired because something illegal was found in her bag. I took all of this with a grain of salt because I did not know the real circumstances. I was also told about a week later that Esmerelda was back. I was told that she was in some way related to a tribal member who threatened to sue Harrah's. I also noticed that Esmerelda had been P/T and was now full-time. What disturbed me was that I had never done anything that would bring me close to being fired; however, I was not offered a full-time position.

I decided to ask at least one guest to let my supervisor know so that I could have an outside level of service viewpoint. I had a 7-Star and her companion who were very upset. Apparently, the companion was unable to verify that he was a companion and they would not let him in the Diamond Lounge. The 7-Star complained that she was tired of having to leave her machine and go to verify him all the time. I checked their ID's and both of their accounts. They were both listed as joint-accounts. However, I, neither the 7-Star, did not know at the time that Cherokee had changed the policy whereby a 7-Star had to renew the companion each year. This was not the same as the joint-account. In my zeal to please them (as with the Host Cash), I printed out the F3 screen for them on their respective accounts. This way, the companion could show to the Diamond Lounge that he was a 7-Star Companion. After they left, I was told that this was not something I was supposed to do. Linda told me about the new policy. I didn't understand at first why they couldn't have a copy of their own information. Linda told me that technically it's not the guest's information; it's ours. Also, I'd forgotten about the C.A.P. information on the sheet. Linda said they may ask their representative about it. A guest isn't even supposed to know about it. However, I have had a 7-Star come to me once and wanted to know what his C.A.P. score was and I told him I couldn't give out that information. He wasn't happy about this and said he would just ask his representative. Linda told Ethel about what happened and I offered to retrieve the sheets from the guests. They said I could do this if the guests were compliant and I had a good rapport with them. Linda told her that the male companion had thanked me and told Linda what a great job I had done. In fact, the 7-Star said that she was going to tell everyone to go to Rachel in TR if they needed to get anything done. So, it was "bittersweet" to say the least. Nevertheless, I learned that this part was not entered into my Personnel Log File.

I retrieved the sheets from the guests. They were very gracious and consenting and had never even noticed anything about the C.A.P. or even inquired about it. I did not receive a write-up; however, I was told it would be noted in my file. At this point, I realized it was best if I kept better documentation on an almost-daily basis.

June 27 – I applied for the VIP Host and Special Events & Promotions Supervisor position. I left them with Jack to be signed. Ethel told me later that day that Jack had left something for me. The signed transfer applications were in a manila envelope. He had put N/A for 90-day evaluation, 3 points for attendance, and "no" for having taken Superlap.

Chapter 9

Blowing Off Steam

June 29 – Came into work to get my coupons. Ethel, Jack, and Zelda were in the room. I received the schedule for the next week and was very surprised and angry. I noticed that Beverly, along with many others in the department, were now full-time. I stated that I was angry, even "pissed" because of this. I told them that I almost never use that word. I was determined to talk to Felicia about it; however, I saw Ivan before I saw Felicia. Since he had told me I could come to him, I stated that I was very angry and dejected about it. He tried to explain to me how they arrived at their decisions. When I went down to the Rotunda, I asked Victoria if she felt I had been doing a good job for the past 90 days and she told me she thought I had. I asked her why Beverly was full-time and not me. She said she would be curious to know also. When asked by another co-worker how I was, I told them I was angry. However, another co-worker (Carrie) told me she was upset and I told her I knew exactly what she was going to say before she said it. She too was upset that Beverly had received full-time with great hours. However, Carrie was upset because she had turned down the full-time position because she was told only sunrise shift was available. When Felicia came in, I told her I would like to talk with her when she had time. It was later that I was called into a meeting with Ivan and Felicia. Ivan told me that they created a matrix with various criteria and measured each employee. However, it seems not every supervisor's input was included in the matrix. I was told that several other employees scored higher than I did. I told Ivan that I disagreed because I knew that I had been doing an excellent job. I also realize that the matrix comparison was comparing apples and oranges. I say this because you cannot compare employees who have not spent the same amount of time in a position. An employee who has been in a job longer has had more time to make more mistakes, as compared with an employee who has been there only a short time. In addition, as of June 1, our department no longer re-wrote coupons for guests. It is this area that gave our department the most problems. Ivan told me that he had been manager for 10 years and that he was not going to change the way he runs the department for anyone. This is interesting for him to say this because I discovered that our department scored in the bottom 25%. I was told that I could go to HR and be reassigned if need be. I told him that we could agree to disagree. I know that disagreement does not mean non-compliance. Just because we disagree does not mean we don't adhere to what we're supposed to do. When I asked if I could see the matrix and see how I stacked up against my peers, Ivan told me that I could not, that I could only see how I scored. I have not received this and I still have not received my 90-day evaluation. Ivan told me that the 90-day is informal and not written. I told him that even though I was angry, the guests were never aware of it. He said, yes, but my co-workers were. They were only aware because I told them, not because I acted like it. He said that we all have problems and should leave them at the door. The only problem I had presented itself after I came through the door. However, I told Ivan that I am not affected by the attitudes and dispositions of my co-workers and that I have intrinsic motivation for my job. When I asked to know what I should be doing better or stop doing, he said it was not their job to help me do my job better and they only need to supply me with the tools to do my job. He asked if I would be OK for that night, and I was surprised by the question, but told him I would be fine. I told him that my daughter and I always pray about our problems. He allowed me to take a 10-minute break before going back to the front line and he talked with Felicia behind closed doors after that. Victoria asked me if I had my talk with Felicia and I just shook my head "yes." Eunice asked me how I was doing, and I said, "I have nothing to say." I was a bit shaken and depressed after this and did not give my usually over-the-top service. I prayed about this later that night and had to remind myself that I always do everything to the glory of God and will not stop doing so. I intend to always give my best service and do the best in whatever I'm given to do, as always.

July 1 – I was in a good mood because I chose to be. When asked how I was doing by a co-worker, I responded: "It's a great day to be alive and a child of the Most High God!"

I saw Natasha several times. I informed her that I had applied for the VIP Host position. She seemed overjoyed, except when I told her I hadn't heard anything yet.

July 2 – I talked briefly with Helen in HR and told her I wasn't being treated very well in Total Rewards and that I hadn't received my 90-day evaluation, even though I'd asked several times for it. I asked her about the Table Games training. She said I could apply for a transfer but that it did not have to be Table Games. I also told her that people have said I should go to Employee Relations. I told her that I had been around the block and worked for many years in several different avenues and capacities and have learned that even when you go to Employee Relations, you still end up getting the "shaft." So, I was very reluctant. I told her that because I was not a tribal member, I felt that I really had no recourse. Even so, I tried contacting ER several times and left messages. I also left messages for Olga in HR to find out the status of the VIP Host position.

Chapter 10

A Ray of Hope

July 3 - I received a call from Personnel to interview for the Sr. Account Executive Host position. They scheduled me for an interview on Thursday at 11am. I start my shift at 12pm and hope the interview will not last past that time.

I created a "Level of Service Inquiry" form that I wanted to suggest to be used in Total Rewards. I had mentioned something like this to Ethel during my initial interview for the Total Rewards Rep position. She had mentioned to me that we were making the guests work too hard to give suggestions and/or comments by not providing something like this to them.

I've been making calls to Employee Relations and leaving messages. I believe they have returned my call on two occasions, but I did not call them back yet. I was told by a co-worker that going to Employee Relations could impact your ability to transfer to another position. I was told by another co-worker how a person in another department was unable to transfer because the person's manager did not want the person to do so. I was not aware they had this much power.

July 4 – I had an interview with Delilah and Sam in Marketing for the Sr. Account Executive Casino Host position.

July 5 – I went up to the 3rd Floor to drop off a thank you card for both Delilah and Sam. I gave the card to the secretary at the desk and saw Ivan. He asked if I was looking for him. I said hello to him and told him that I was actually looking for Delilah. I asked Ivan how he was doing that day and I left.

Later that evening, Felicia, my supervisor met with me and asked me if I had seen my Personnel file. I told her I had not. She showed me the electronic file and told me that I could look at it whenever I wanted to do so. She told me that they document everything and went over each point with me. I noticed that many of my positives were not entered. However, I made no comments verbally except to tell her that I remembered certain events. I noticed that Ivan had not accurately entered in his comments in the meeting I had with him and Felicia. In fact, it was misrepresented and/or missing what he actually said to me in the meeting.

July 6 – I was told by a co-worker that there were productivity sheets in the Buzz Area of Total Rewards and that it had each of the TR reps listed and how we measured up. On my break, I looked for them on the board when we first walk in, but I did not find it where the co-worker said it was located. I saw Linda and she showed me where they were. I guess they had always been there but I never noticed them, nor knew they were there. In fact, none of the supervisors even mentioned them during our Buzz sessions. I only viewed the June report because it was on top and because that's all I had time to look at. The left column was the Efficiency. I believe I was listed as number 8 or 9. Linda said it had to do with how many reps were on shift at that particular location. She said the people who worked the sunrise shifts were always at the top because there were fewer people. I noticed that Tilly was #1 and Beverly was #2. Linda also told me that people assisting a 7-Star and Diamond counted more heavily than when assisting other guests. Now I realize why Beverly always wanted to sit in the Diamond Chair. Since she is Jack's niece, she was probably already aware of the weighted measurement. The other side of the sheet listed number of transactions for the month. I was amazed to see that I had over 4,000 transactions that month and that I was #3, just under Leslie who was #1 and Barbara who was #2. I also took into account that not everybody goes back and checks the information to make sure it is updated and the fact that I am more than twice their age. These numbers bothered me a bit because they appeared to mean nothing when Ivan and his group decided that I didn't quite "measure up" above the newer employees whereby they were given full-time positions instead of me.

Chapter 11
Good News Travels Fast

July 7 – We were told by Ethel during Buzz that there has been a lot of gossip in the department and that she was "tired of it." She said that if you were doing it, to stop, and that if you were listening to it, don't. One co-worker said she would listen if the person wanted to talk and told her to go talk to her supervisor. Ethel said that we shouldn't even say this and just tell the person we "didn't want to hear it" and let them go talk to a counselor or something. I wasn't exactly sure to what she was referring but she kept saying that we should be talking about more positive things like what's going on with our grandchildren. The fact that she said "grandchildren" made me know that she was talking to the reps my age, even though there were others in Buzz at the time who were obviously too young to have grandchildren. I told them that I was upset "one day" and that I heard about it later (meaning Ivan said this to me in the meeting with him and Felicia). I told them that I told myself, "I can't say that anymore." Ethel said that it was a great department and that if we weren't happy, we should transfer out. It was interesting that she would say this because I know she knew I had already completed transfer papers for several positions. One co-worker told me later that it seemed it was OK when people were gossiping about her and about me, but when people were talking about the incident with Esmerelda, all of a sudden it was a big problem. In Ethel's defense, I do agree that the gossip needed to be curtailed. However, sometimes staff did need to talk about their problems with someone they could trust. I should know because I've done my share of counseling.

My daughter and I learned that one of our co-workers who lived next door to us was found dead in her apartment. The previous day a neighbor had been knocking and knocking on her door. We then saw the Sheriff go to the door and do the same thing for a long time. We were told that they believe she committed suicide with drugs. Apparently, she had been very depressed, even though she had just gotten back from going to her son's wedding. Her son lives out of state. This very incident is one reason people at work need to have someone to talk to.

July 9 – Felicia met with me to read over a long email that Ethel had received from Vera, one of the people I had talked to at the Front Desk on yesterday while trying to get a $75 Stay & Play approved for a guest who came up to me. Vera said that my tone was "frantic" and that she wanted my supervisor to talk to me because she "hated to think Rachel would talk to a guest that way." I told Felicia about the situation and how the guest was upset because she had already gone through a hassle upstairs and was sent down to TR. I was on the phone for quite a while trying to get the verification and had talked to two reps before finally getting Vera who is the one who made the reservation for the guest. I told the reps the guest was not on the list I was given and that I needed the 6- to 7-digit account – otherwise we would receive a $75 variance if we swiped the guest's TR card and it turned out she was not authorized. I had gone through this type of process on 4 other occasions. Also, because I was on the phone for a longer time, the line was filling up with guests. My tone was straightforward and there was a sense of urgency; however, I was by no means rude. Vera asked if I had asked my supervisor lately for a new sheet. I told her I hadn't and would do so. I put the phone down and went and asked Linda who checked her email and printed out the new sheet. Linda had been very busy also. I got the information and told Vera that we did have the information. I thanked her before I got off the phone. I then confirmed the guest and gave her the coupons. I told Felicia that "I give up" and that it "seems like no matter what I do people have a problem with it." Felicia told me not to worry about it.

Muriel had me sign a spotlight from Felicia. Muriel said that "of course everything is top-box."

I noticed that I'm still being scheduled for 36-38 hours even though I'm still part-time. However, I've heard from other co-workers that the part-timers will be scheduled for no more than 30 hours per week real soon.

Barbara said that she read that all staff was responsible for getting change for a guest while on the floor. She asked Felicia about it who thought the same thing. I told them that in my New Employee Orientation I was told that Total Rewards reps do not handle cash. Felicia said she would check on it. She either asked Victoria or Victoria overhead her. Victoria said that no, we were never supposed to do that. Then they both decided that we could sit and hold a machine for them while they went to get change or wait for a casino host.

I am still hearing reports from co-workers that a manager can actually stop a person from transferring out of their department. I know this has got to be against company policy. Barbara told me and Tilly that she was surprised that she had gotten full-time. She said that nobody told her and that she had not even "asked for it." I told her to be thankful because I asked for it and didn't get it. She said that she had until July 21st to accept it because it had come in the mail. I didn't show it to her but the nagging feeling of being rejected for no good reason and done an injustice and disservice welled up inside me. I've played poker for many years and have a good poker face. When in front of guests and others I can be upbeat and positive because I'm determined to be so. I made myself not comment any further, nor did I mention to anyone at work about the email from Vera.

Chapter 12

Dejection and Rejection

July 10 – I was told that they would make a decision about the Sr. Acct Exec Casino Host position by Monday, but I still had not heard anything. I called HR and was told that a specific HR rep handled that position. She transferred me to her extension and I left a voice mail. My guess was that I had not been selected and just wanted to verify it. I still had not heard about my application for the VIP Host or Special Events & Promotions Supervisor position. It is still bothering me as to how I have been tossed aside in Total Rewards when I'm more qualified than most of the people there. I know I have to contact Employee Relations again. I know that this will negatively impact my ability to get another position at Cherokee, even though it's not supposed to. I kept thinking how Caesars made a stand on the issue with Paula Deen and that hopefully they will understand and hopefully do something about the fact that I feel I have been discriminated against because of my race, age, and gender – everything that makes me a Black woman and considered low on the Totem Pole in our society today.

July 11 – I was scheduled to work 6 hours from 12:00pm to 6pm. Jack asked me if I had lived for a long time in Arizona. I told him yes, that I had taught at the Gila River Indian Community for 3 years. He said that he wasn't aware of the poverty that existed in the mid-West. I told him that it was pretty bad. I asked if I was going down to the Rotunda and he said that I was going upstairs. There were only two other reps when I got up there; however, more came later. On duty there were Alexis, Lena, Esmerelda, Jeffrey, Mona, and Louise. During the shift, I only saw Jack come upstairs once and Edward came up once to talk to Jeffrey. Edward told him that he was talking to everyone. I noticed that Alexis and Esmerelda were eating Skittles. I noticed that Louise was chewing gum the whole time she was there; it was very evident. I was on the very end to the right. I noticed that not very often did most of the reps stand up when a guest was in line like we were instructed to do. Also, even though guests were down at the farthest end from me, I had to wait on them because some of the other reps were not standing or sitting and talking. I found the whole situation very unprofessional. I didn't understand why two of these reps were written up for excellent customer service in the little magazine I'd seen lying around. Most people I find there are only "on" when supervisors are around. The worst part is when I went on break to the Motor Coach area, I saw Louise who was still chewing gum, coming out of the door and I saw Ivan standing in there and Ethel was counting out money. They apparently had been laughing about something because I asked them if they were having a party. There could have been no way that Ivan and/or Ethel did not notice that Louise had been chewing gum. I mention this because everything little thing I do is noted in my Personnel file while others seem to get away with "murder."

July 12 – I had left messages with Phoebe in HR to find out about the Senior Acct Executive Casino Host position for which I applied. She never returned my calls, so I tried calling Delilah. I got her voice mail but left no message. I thought it odd that the front desk person usually never asks me "who's calling"; however, she did when I asked for Delilah. I asked why she needed to know this and she said so she can tell her who's calling. When I said that she'd never asked me this before, she was "short" and told me that she would just transfer me. I called Phoebe again until I reached her. She said that the last time she talked to the Marketing Dept. they had not made a final decision. I also asked her about the VIP Host and Special Events and Promotions Supervisor positions because I had been told she was handling those positions now instead of Olga. She told me that the VIP Host position had been filled. I didn't understand because I didn't get an interview. She said that the internal position had gone to an "01." She said that I must have applied for the external position after it had closed. I told her that I had already tried applying externally for the position the first time. When I learned that we needed to apply internally I tried to apply for it but I was given a different listing that did not have the VIP Host position listed. I explained that Olga told me previously that she would correct the position title and send my application (transfer papers) over to the department. However, the fact that they called me to interview for the Sr. Acct Exec. Casino Host position tells me that she never did this. I was also told that if the VIP Host position is posted again and that I could apply again by calling her (Olga) or her manager to let them know I was still interested. I was extremely disappointed and felt this whole process was confusing and very unprofessional. None of the positions have a closing date behind them. How is an employee or anyone else supposed to know? I felt that something was not quite "kosher" and that I was being given the runaround. Phoebe also told me that the hiring department for the Special Events & Promotions Supervisor position were still going over the applications and had not started interviewing. By now I am depressed and dismayed and realize that I may have been "black listed" (pun intended).

When I came to work I noticed that the internal posting was listed with several jobs. I noticed that the VIP Host position was listed, along with Total Rewards Representative. Phoebe had told me that the positions are updated every Friday. This still confused me because it makes no sense that I was not interviewed when I applied both externally and internally for the VIP Host position. It seems that they do things to find ways to hire an "01" over other employees and I know this is Tribal Law; however, everything has been done to my detriment even when I was not up against an "01." Also, I discovered that there was a notice on the TR bulletin board that Lance had received the Dual Rate Supervisor position. I was glad for him; however, I had heard that Brad thought he would get the position. Even though I had heard this, I overhead Muriel tell Lance, "I hear that congratulations are in order" two weeks prior to this. I felt that this was to what she was referring but I was not sure until today. I realize that the Total Rewards Rep position that was posted was listed to replace Lance. This depressed me even more because they still never offered me a full-time position yet here they were listing a full-time position on the internal job listings. I saw that Carrie was a bit depressed and down also. I realized then and there that it was to an employee's detriment to have a supervisor sign off when an employee wanted to apply for a different position other than their own department. This is the only company that I have worked for that has done this. I was told by Helen that they do this so that the manager will be aware that there might be an opening in their department so that they know how to plan. If an employee is mandated to give at least 2 weeks' notice before starting another position, this is enough time for a manager to plan. This would be the same thing if an employee left to go to another company. Also, when an employee is terminated for good reason or "pointed out" the manager would still find him or her in the position of having a vacancy abruptly. When I asked an HR rep if the current process would damage your relationship with your own department, she said that if it did, you could go to Employee Relations.

Chapter 13

Most Desirable Employer in NC?

Leslie's roommate came to the Rotunda and told Linda that Leslie had a life-threatening surgery that day and she gave her paperwork because Leslie wanted to make sure she didn't lose her job. She said that the doctor said Leslie would be out for about 11 days. Her friend was very frantic and I tried to get her to calm down. I told her that it would be all right. I asked if Leslie would be OK and she said she would be now. What type of company puts a point system in place that does not allow for an employee to be ill without being in jeopardy of losing his or her job? The company loses so many good employees who fall by the wayside because of this. However, when you are the only casino that is surrounded by four other states without a casino, you can pretty much do what you want.

It is my guess that either the Tribe or the state of North Carolina pays the state of Georgia, Tennessee, South Carolina, and Virginia not to have casinos so that they can have this type of monopoly, power, and control. I have invested in Caesar's Entertainment stock. I bought it at 14.00 and have seen it go up to 16.00 within a few days. It is my guess that the stand they took on Paula Deen was a good PR move.

I was told that the casino was charging for the preliminaries for the Ultimate Elvis Contest this year. I heard that it was a success last year but they had only sold 400 tickets this year for an event center that seats 3000. We've been promoting the $150,000 free slot play giveaway for tomorrow. It is my guess that not many will show up because of the way the promotion was handled for the Saturday giveaway last month. I haven't understood why they give only a few prizes away in such large amounts instead of spreading out the wealth. This is bad business in my book. It works on the same principal as charging exorbitantly high prices for an item whereby you may get fewer sales because not everyone is able to afford to buy it – as opposed to selling an item at an affordable price whereby you get a multitude of sales and continual sales. I also noticed that a lot of the regulars have stopped coming because corporate no longer allows TR to reprint coupons for them. I like doing this for them. I'm sure someone decided that our production would improve if we did not do this. People seemed excited about the Hidden Jackpot promotion. A great number of them have been winning between $5 and $500 free slot play when they swipe their rewards card between noon and 8pm. We're still getting a great number of new card holders.

I've noticed that a lot of guests want to give tips to us at TR. We tell them that we're not allowed to take them and the guests seem disappointed. I always tell them to give a tip to the Cage Cashiers because they don't seem to get many tips. For me, this is unusual because the other casinos in Arizona are run a bit differently. Their cage cashiers always get lots of tips and they allow their employees to play poker when not on duty. However, they are not allowed to play slots.

I've noticed that several employees who have been lauded for their customer service skills are actually not good employees, not friendly to staff, and have stated how they "hate" the guests. I find this extremely ironic. I'm not very impressed with Ivan as a manager; however, I saw him listed as one of the people nominated for a Q2 Leadership Award. I also learned that he is the manager of both TR and Valet. Now it makes sense why the sunrise shift at TR gives out the valet keys when Valet closes. I did not understand this before.

Arnette sent me an email that she was told by Ethel that she could not give out her Christian cards to anyone at work because this was "soliciting." Apparently one of the employees complained. It's always interesting that anything of God is seen as soliciting; however, my daughter has told me that there is a link to the Gay & Lesbian website at the bottom of Cherokee's website.

Felicia asked me if I'd seen my picture up in the Buzz area. I told her I hadn't noticed. She said it's at the "very top."

I am very tired because I'd worked myself silly since we were so busy all day long. Felicia comes in later and does not always see what I do. I'm usually filling up the bins with "bungee" cords, putting the used TR cards from guests in the recycle bin, and filling the bins with new cards as needed. Sometimes we were so busy that I didn't have time to do it. I was tired and my back hurt, however, I was the one Felicia asked to fill the bins with new cards when it seemed like a lull. It's really not fair to her or to me for her to be my supervisor; however, I believe her to be a pretty good supervisor, even though she is new in the role after being a D/R supervisor to Ethel.

I told Felicia that I would love to leave early when she asked me. I noticed that we were again scheduled with far too many staff than we needed on the front line. I was glad to leave early since I wasn't feeling well.

July 13 – It's Saturday so it was real busy in the casino. During Buzz, I hugged and congratulated Lance on his new position as D/R Supervisor. I playfully asked him if this meant I would have to stop disrespecting him now. He laughed and told me not to stop anything that I was doing. Beverly told me she was working 10 hours that day. I had 29 people request $5 free slot play, a great others chose the Buy One, Get One Free Buffet, and only a few chose the $5 Food Credit and 15% off Retail Shops. I had previously typed up a sheet with the 4 options for the guests to look at so they would have time to make a decision and didn't feel rushed, and this also saved some of my voice, since I have so much to tell new guests. Haven't seen many of the regulars from March, April, or May. The $150,000 free slot play giveaway brought tons of people in, including new people. People were excited about winning between $5 and $500 in free slot play instantly when they swiped their card at the kiosk and to be put into the drawing for the $150,000 at 10pm. Since you had to swipe your card by 9pm, a great deal of people had been misinformed and were still swiping their cards after 9pm, thinking they would be included in the drawing. Felicia said they should time the kiosks to go off when the swiping no longer applied.

I ended up at the farthest end most of the day. Even when the 7-Star seat is available, I don't sit in it unless I have to. I feel I've been demeaned by not being offered a full-time position and made to feel I'm not up to par to my peers, which could be further from the truth because I always give 110%. However, I notice that Barbara doesn't hesitate to sit in the 7-Star chair. I worked so hard that my lower back hurt. Linda asked if I was all right. I told her about my back and she asked me if I had ever gone to a chiropractor. I told her that I had and that my daughter used to work for one. I know that I can't keep working at this pace much longer. I've worked for very hard most of my life. I know that if anyone else with my skills, abilities, education, background, who was not a Black female and/or not my age, they would be further along in their career. Sometimes I feel that I should never have left Gila River Indian community. That was the most money I'd ever made in my life working for someone else. However, because like everything else, no one wants to promote me because of what I look like or because of my age, or because of a combination of the three – my age, gender, and race – I have always sought out my own business.

I had zero-variance again. They have taught me that they are unforgiving of my mistakes, so I make sure I don't make them anymore. Ethel's comment was: "Perfect!" I noticed that Linda may have had a variance; I wasn't sure. She was in uniform that day and on the front line. Also, I believe Linda said she was 1-1/2 hours late to work because she forgot her badge and had to go back and get it. It was a day when we had to park in the lot. Victoria bragged that she had forgotten her badge and still got to work with 5 minutes to spare. She said that in 8 years she had never had to wear an "I forgot my badge" badge, and she wasn't about to start.

Chapter 14

A Caring Community?

I've been hearing about so much corruption at the casino. I'd been told that cage cashiers and casino hosts have been keeping back thousands of dollars and, subsequently, have been fired. However, the money is never recovered. I've been hearing how co-workers have been having sex with each other, sometimes while on duty. One younger co-worker shot and killed another older co-worker. The two had been dating and in a serious relationship. However, something went awry, ending in the death of the younger one (female). Apparently she had been shot in the face several times. I'm told that the Table Games Dept. is the worst. I'm told there is a "clique" and if you're not in it, you don't stand a chance to get anywhere. I've been told that the table games dealers feel they are the "cream of the crop" and bring in the most revenue, so they feel they are above the other employees. I don't know if this is true because I don't work with them; however, I only know a few of them. I notice that there are about 4 Black women who are table games dealers. Only one is a supervisor, I believe. I have yet to see any Black woman at Cherokee who came up through the ranks and in a managerial position. However, there are Black men who are VIP Hosts and supervisors. In fact, there are a lot of them.

Arnette was excited. She showed me her paper that appeared to be confirmation for her. She sent me an email about it. I was so happy for her. God is truly amazing! It seems God is blessing others; however, I'm still waiting for mine. Sometimes I feel as though he's forgotten about me.

I like TR because you learn a lot and have access to a great deal of information. However, I know I'm not being treated fairly. There has got to be a better way to put bread on one's table. The hard part is I applied for so, so many jobs in Georgia and with the County in North Carolina. I received no interviews whatsoever. It became apparent to me after a while that I was not getting hired because of my age. No company wanted to hire someone who was a few years from being 60 years old. Why is my life like this? God, please help me understand this. Where are you? I thought the Hebrew Israelites were the chosen ones and the apple of your eye. My tears overflow like rivers at home. However, at work, none of them know how much pain I'm in. I am still upbeat and positive with the guests and with my co-workers. I know that my Father in Heaven will work everything out for my good. I leave all my problems in his hands and will wait for his leading as to when, how, and where I am to go and what I am to do.

Chapter 15

The Way We Do Things

July 14 – During Buzz, Eunice was upset because of what was going on with her daughter and a friend of hers. She was very vocal and told Ethel and the other reps there about what happened. She said she felt like she'd been through the wringer. Not once did Ethel say anything about not having an UPA, but commented and asked her questions. Ethel said to me: "Kids are a handful, aren't they Rachel?" I told her that my daughter is always a sweetheart but I was glad my son was finally married. She said she only had one daughter and that she was pretty good. Ethel told me to send Mona back to be counted out and that when Eunice arrived, we could send Maxine back. I notice that we have a few people with the same first names in the department, one of which is a D/R supervisor.

It was not real busy but we did have guests come in intermittently. Victoria had come in at 2pm; Jeffrey said he would be leaving at 7:30pm, Carol would be leaving in about an hour. I ended up sitting in the Diamond chair and eventually in the 7-Star chair when Linda came on duty. Arnette came down to the Rotunda briefly to work. We laughed about her confirmation again. She was in a good mood. I talked briefly with Linda (in the back) about the run around I was being given with the VIP Host position. I told her I'd been interviewed for the Sr. Acct. Exec. Casino Host position and that I expected not to be hired, but hadn't heard the final word yet. I asked her about the full-time position that was posted internally for the TR Rep. She said she thinks it's to encourage everyone to go full-time. I said that it didn't make any sense that they wouldn't offer it to me. She told me to speak to Jack about it. I questioned whether I should speak to Jack instead of Felicia who was my supervisor and she said yes, that I should speak to Jack. She said to ask him if there was a way I could apply for the position or if it was something that could be handled internally. She said for me to talk to him right away before someone else does. She also told me that it was HR who came up with the matrix, and by using it, they were able to allow the new people to get the full-time positions, instead of going by seniority. I still have not seen the matrix. I shared with her that I felt it might be hurting me because I did apply for a transfer in order to apply for the other positions. She said that it was possible but that she didn't know. She shared with me her experiences with talking with Vince who is Ivan's boss. She said it was not a positive encounter. She also told me about how she had met with HR and was very angry a few years ago and tried her best to understand why she was not being hired and/or promoted. She said she believed it had to do with her age but also you had to be a person who didn't say much and didn't make waves. She asked me how many points I had and I said "2." She said I should be fine. She said she had 5 points now and that she couldn't transfer out even if she wanted to do so.

I noticed that the casino was very busy yet not many people were standing in the cashier lines. Also, there weren't very many people winning jackpots that I could tell. One casino host came up to get a card for a guest who had won a jackpot. Apparently, the guest had not previously acquired a TR card prior to winning the jackpot.

I remember the first time I'd seen an alert on a guest's account. It would not allow me to print a card for the guest. I showed it to Muriel and she said it was not a problem. She called the casino manager and printed out the guest's F3 screen with all of the messages and told me to print out the screen with all of her personal info. The guest gave us her license and social security card. It was 11:30 pm and the guest was concerned that her free cash coupon for $150 would expire before she could redeem it at the cashier. After a while I was able to print her card (she was a Diamond).

Muriel told her we would find where she was playing and make sure she got her license and social security card. She came back 5 minutes later and said they wouldn't let her redeem it because she didn't have her license. I told her I'd forgotten about that. Finally, the casino manager came back and gave her back her cards. When she left, the casino manager whispered something to Muriel about what the real problem was with the guest, but I didn't hear just what he said.

While in the 7-Star chair, I assisted one of the Black female guests who was a Diamond player and seemed very grateful that I'd exceeded her expectations in helping her and telling her about her Diamond Celebration Dinner. I asked her if she would send in either an email or letter to Total Rewards about the service I'd provided. I told her that I rarely have guests who do that. She said she would. I told Linda about it and she said again how the other reps do self-promotion quite a bit. I asked if they had been told to do that and she said that they just did it on their own.

When Charles came down to the Rotunda, he told me about the big fiasco they had in the Motor Coach area. Apparently the people on the bus had been issued coupons for $20 but they were the wrong date. I guess a Promotions Rep had to get them replaced from Corporate. Charles said there a bit of confusion but they finally got it straightened out. Later, when I went to be counted out, I noticed that Ethel (I believe) had written on the board a thank you to Nicholas, Alexis, Louise, Esmerelda, and Jack and put in parentheses that they knew why they were being thanked. This was great; however, it's still amazing to me that they get lauded for things like this but never reprimanded for the things I encountered while there three days ago when they were chewing gum, eating candy, not standing up for guests, etc. My morale is starting to dwindle even more because of things like this.

I notice that Carol is not as spirited as usual. Though I had not talked with her, my guess was she applied for the D/R also but did not receive it because Lance was chosen. Of all the reps, other than Victoria who has been there for 8 years and says she doesn't want a D/R position because she likes to leave her work at home, and Mary who has too many points, Carol seemed to be the most knowledgeable. However, they may have felt she was too young and not authoritative enough for the position.

Arnette said she found a couch but needed a truck to pick it up. I told her about Lance. I told her he'd given me a ride home one night because I couldn't reach my daughter. I told her to talk to him. She said she would.

About 12:17 pm I went back to be counted out even though there were 3 guests in line. I knew that if I didn't go on back that I would be late clocking out. I thought Ethel and/or Linda were back at the Motor Coach area. I didn't find anyone there. I tried using one of the 5 radios but there was no signal on either of them. I waited a few minutes and then started to head back to the Rotunda. I saw Muriel and Eunice coming. I told them that the radios were not working. Muriel asked if I'd clocked out yet and I said I was going to. She told me to go on and clock out. I did so and then back to be counted out. She counted out Eunice first. When she finished counting me out I apologized because I didn't know she was by herself. I told her I thought Ethel and/or Linda were there. She said it was all right and she kidded that they had absconded. I notice that she uses the "sh-word" quite a bit. She's not angry; it's just part of what she says at times but never to a guest.

It seems Ethel never asks me to work in the Motor Coach area. I notice that Barbara, Sean, and maybe Charles have. I've never said I would not work there; I've just said that I like working at the Rotunda. However, I will work happily wherever they send me. It really doesn't matter. I'm the same with the guests wherever I go.

I noticed another young Black female in a suit in the EDR talking with another young Black man in a suit. My guess is that they may be either casino hosts or table games supervisors. I couldn't get close enough to see their badges without being obvious.

Chapter 16

Fighting for What's Right

Week of July 15 (Monday) – I dropped off the following memo to Ivan regarding a full-time position. I keep wondering to myself why I always have to "fight" for everything:

MEMORANDUM

Date: July 15

To: Ivan, TR Manager

From: Rachel, TR Representative

Re: F/T Position

Cc: Felicia, TR Supervisor

This memo is a follow-up to the meeting we had two weeks ago where you answered my complaint about not receiving a full-time position. Since I have been in the department, everything done there has been by seniority. You said you chose to use a matrix this year. I was told by Penny in HR that they have always used a matrix. She said that only the Dept. Manager and the HR Manager are allowed to see the matrix. You told me verbally what the criteria were; however, I would still like to know how I scored. What I mean is, for each item, I would like to know what the highest value is and what my score is. I know that I cannot see the scores of other co-workers due to confidentiality issues.

Please know that I know that I have worked my heart out since I've been in this department. Muriel can attest to this, if asked. I thought that Ethel was aware of this also, but I'm not certain. I did not, until recently, even know about the productivity/statistical sheets that were posted in the Buzz Area. They were never mentioned during Buzz at all. Though I've glanced and seen sheets on the wall, it wasn't until recently that a co-worker told me that all of the reps' names were on the monthly efficiency and volume sheets. I'm not quite sure how these are measured, but I was surprised to see that I was #3 for the number of transactions for the month of June. Even so, the two people just above me, Leslie and Barbara, are more than half my age. The fact that I am able to produce this much should attest to part of my demonstrated ability. In addition, I always notice that a lot of the accounts do not have phone numbers, emails, DL numbers, including State and expiration dates. After printing the card, I always go back into the 41 screen and update the information. I know that I'm good at what I do. In addition, with regard to customer service, I continue to have "Top Box" as a result of my spotlights.

I would like to request a F/T position. Although I stated in March that part-time was fine with me, it was not until later that I realized what being P/T meant: (1) I would no longer have the same seniority since F/T employees have precedence over P/T; (2) I will need medical insurance by next year because of Obamacare. Otherwise, I will incur a federal fine. I have discovered that it is not easy to obtain medical insurance here in North Carolina. (3) I was routinely scheduled for full-time hours for almost my entire 90 days, while still being listed as part-time. I would like the same opportunity for a F/T position that has been given to the many employees who have started after me. (4) A few months ago, Felicia asked me to check on a sheet of paper whether or not I would be interested in a F/T position. I marked the box that said "Yes" I was interested in a F/T position. Felicia stated to me that people hired before me would be considered for F/T positions; based on seniority. She never mentioned that the matrix was a determining factor in deciding an employee's promotion from P/T to F/T position. (5) I know that Lance has been promoted to D/R Supervisor and his shift and hours should be available. I would like to request the F/T position that Lance has vacated, which was swing swift.

I respectfully ask that you consider my request. Thank you.

Good day at work; we're getting more new signups due to the Hidden Jackpot promotion. I redeemed a $500 free slot play for a guest. She said she was on her way to leave and decided to just swipe her card. She was very excited. Ethel asked me if I had big plans for my day off. I told her I had plans to go to Atlanta for Red Lobster. She said her preference would be Asheville rather than go all the way to Atlanta.

Tuesday, July 16th – It's been two weeks since my daughter applied for the Table Games Dealer Training when the position was posted internally. She finally received a call from Lester to go in and take the Math Test. She passed the test of course because she said it simpler than the one we took when we first applied 4 months ago. In the meantime, I asked Helen if I could take the Superlap. She brought me back into the office and input some initial information into the computer. I was surprised when she said I could take the test that day. The test was three parts. The first part was timed and tested your reasoning and logic skills with regard to patterns and shapes whereby you had to determine which diagram, among 5 choices, would be next in the series. I answered 20 out of 30 questions. The second part was not timed and was more of a personality/trait test that Helen said counted for 65% of the test. The third part was timed and was a math test. I answered all of the questions with about 15 minutes to spare. Afterward, Helen told me I passed and that Phoebe would get with me when she got back regarding an interview when she got back from vacation on Monday (July 22nd). I can read body language really well. Helen had sighed. It was as if her manner was saying, "You passed but more than likely it won't help you; however, of course, I can't tell you that."

Of course my daughter passed the math test and Lester called the hiring manager for the Table Games Dealing Training to see if they wanted to interview my daughter. I waited for her in the car outside. When she came back she was in tears. She said it was a group "interview" with a total of 20 people. She said they asked 5 questions which she thought were pretty lame. She said it wasn't even a real interview and the managers were very unprofessional. She said the manager told her that she "wouldn't tell Mildred you're here." The last question/request was for the candidates to "imitate their favorite celebrity." My daughter said the manager looked her square in the face and said that this was the most important question you've answered today. My daughter did a line ("All righty then") from one of Jim Carey's movies. She said there were 4 other people who hardly said very much. She said she did answer questions and talked; however, the other candidates were never really over-the-top bubbly. She said the managers went out and Lester came back in and told her and the other 4 who had not answered the last question to come with him. She said she felt hopeful because maybe the 5 of them were selected for the training school. However, Lester took them back into HR and told them that they would not be offered the position at that time but that they could apply for one of the other open positions. My daughter was devastated because she was the only one there in uniform and who obviously already worked for the casino. She thought sure she would be chosen because it was only dealer training and she and I both had never seen any of the dealers be overly bubbly and over-the-top with the guests. Yes, a few of them were friendly but most are usually sullen and look like they would rather be anywhere else but there. I've even talked to a few of them and had various responses. One told me "It's not what it's cracked up to be." One told me it was a terrible department and that it's who you know. One told me that she liked it and said that there were still openings for the position. Leroy, who was in my New Employee Orientation had been encouraging a few months back and did say that you had to be there at least 90 days before being able to transfer over. My daughter said she was embarrassed because she, having worked in the casino for 4 months and had chip and cash handling experience already, was more qualified than the other 19 who had never worked in the casino before. It still remains to be seen, however, whether some of the chosen 15 had worked for other casinos. My guess is that they had not. The very next day Harrah's was having a job fair to recruit more individuals for the external positions. My daughter said that her manager may have had something to do with her not being able to transfer. She said that Cliff, one of the cage cashiers who had been there for quite a while keeps getting rejected when he applies. He has told me daughter that they won't let him "out of the cage." This is a good example of why your department should not be allowed to know when you apply and interview for another position. It seems that most of the other employees know how to play the game. They try to make sure they have the position even before they apply. This is easy to accomplish through networking. Also, Carrie, one of the other TR reps and tribal member, told me she had the Income Control position (internal) for $11/hour even before she officially put in her transfer papers. I remember hearing Poindexter, another TR rep who is a tribal member, telling her to put in for the position. A tribal member can pretty much get any position they want if they meet the minimum qualifications and haven't been put on someone's "not-to-do list."

Chapter 17

Backsliding

Since my daughter was pretty distraught and in my misguided efforts to cheer her up, I suggested we go play poker in Jacksonville. She quickly agreed. The fact that we left the small black bag at home with all of our toiletries was a clear sign that the time would be a disaster. I suggest that if you must go to the casino that you never, ever just go to the casino on a whim. You should always plan out your trip. Most people like this type of spontaneity but it can usually turn out to be a mistake. This was a disastrous repeat of another time we went to Jacksonville when we were in Georgia. It was only a 5 hour drive then; this time it was almost 8 hours because we got stopped by the North Georgia police. It was evening time and the Black police officer told us that we need to get a light put on our back license plate because Florida police were real stringent about that. However, we passed by several Florida policeman who never bothered us. I don't know if the aftermath of the acquittal of George Zimmerman and the ensuing marches by angry protesters had anything to do with it or not.

Now, together we had saved up some money so we could pay IRS and continue to build up the business. Even though I wasn't sure what I wanted to do exactly. I wasn't sure if I wanted to continue with the business consulting or do employment placement or just focus on marketing my books. It didn't matter; we lost a total of $1,500 for the entire trip. This included transportation and room accommodations, food, and gambling losses. We got to play different games besides Hold'em; we got to play Omaha Hi/Lo and Stud. We lost the most on the Stud because it wasn't Hi/Lo; only Stud High. It seems whenever we're doing well on the Omaha, they do not like to see two Black women winning. It's as if the evil spirit enters into them and/or the devil will send a different person to the table who will change the whole dynamic. Players who were playing tight will start playing loose and calling everything because the player is trying to create action by raising and re-raising pre-flop. We should know by now to leave the table when this starts to happen. It may not be just against Black women; I think it's against women in general. We should have stopped after the first day but we stayed overnight and went back the next day. We did make sure we had gas home, food, and did not lose bill payments because we weren't playing with bill money. However, I hate losing even $100, let alone $1,500. It was such a waste. You never think about it until it's over. Such is the life of gambling.

The Jacksonville trip had been a spur of the moment trip. We had originally planned to take a trip to Ohio and spend a week and had even requested PTO (Paid Time Off) for it. However, we had to rescind our PTO requests. My daughter told me later that she had run the numbers and felt we could still go to the Limit Omaha H/Lo and Limit HORSE Tournaments coming up in August. I told her I would think about it. It's costly. For both of us to play both tournaments at a cost of $220 each would run us up to $980. I told her I'd have to really pray about it. Even if the prize pot, should we manage somehow to win, is in the thousands, I don't know if it would be worth it. I told her that maybe she would have to play and I would watch. However, I don't know if I would have the discipline. If we did go, we would have to make sure we don't have access to any other money. Not sure how we could accomplish this while still being able to allow for emergencies, but we could work it out. It still remains to be seen and I haven't made a decision yet.

Thursday, July 18 – I was scheduled to come in at 12 noon; I wasn't feeling well, so I called in for an EDO (Emergency Day Off). Since it was not the weekend or a mandatory day, I was told there would be no points added. I did not know there was a new callout number. I called the Blind Man's Bluff and they transferred me to a TR Supervisor. I spoke with Edward. My daughter is full-time and she took both of her EDO's back-to-back. I discovered a week later that although no points are added, your date to have your next point rolled off would re-start the day of your EDO. Where I originally had one more month to have a point rolled off, I would not have to wait 2 more months. This didn't bother me because I only had 2 points.

Friday, July 19 – My daughter had not received her schedule and discovered they had scheduled her to come in at 11 in the morning instead of her usual swing/sunrise 4-10's. She was very distraught with everyone and everything because they had not talked with her about having her schedule changed. She had called in the night before and discovered this. She was told by one of the supervisors, "Well, at least you don't have to worry about working past 12 midnight. My daughter had previously requested, in writing, from Wayland, one of the managers, to allow her to come in from 2pm to 12pm. She had never received any response although several weeks had passed by. My daughter was not feeling well; however, I begged her not to take the day off because she would get 3 points. She was not in a good frame of mind because of what had happened the day before and now having her schedule changed, so she stayed home. She was contemplating either letting them fire her or just quitting. She also said that she had stated that she wasn't too keen on working in the Poker Room cage cashier area because it was very slow. My daughter likes to keep busy, especially since the cashiers all have to stand during their entire shift. She said that she heard that Wayland wanted to give you the opposite of what you want, and she felt this is what was happening. They scheduled her to work in the Poker Room for 3 days and at the West Cage one day and the High Limits the other day. She said that all three locations are usually not very busy, especially in the mornings.

Tonight was the Miranda Lambert concert. People seemed to enjoy it even though it was only an hour long. The tickets were expensive and it was standing room only. Two reps from Promotions were at the far end of our area since they were running the 777 Slot Tournament until about 7pm. They usually post the names of the winners in a glass display on the counter when the tournament is over. There are usually 6 winners. It was packed in the casino and we were very busy. I didn't know if very many people were winning jackpots. There were a lot of people wearing boots because of the Miranda Lambert concert. We did get a great deal of new signups. Of course, the $5 free slot play is still the most popular.

It seems my schedule is pretty consistent: Fridays 6pm-2:30am; Saturday – Monday 4m – 12:30pm; Thursday, 12pm – 6pm (38 hours), just 2 hours shy of 40 hours so they can keep me part-time.

Chapter 18

Chills and Thrills

Arnette told me that Jack had said something to her that bothered her in her spirit. She was reluctant to talk about it at work. I asked her to call me.

Felicia called me in and told me that Ivan said they were going to have some more full-time positions and if I was still interested. I told her yes. She asked if I would take any shift, I said yes, because I know if I didn't, I wouldn't get it all. Even if they do give me full-time, I feel as though I'm still getting the shaft because I had seniority over Beverly who has better hours than I do. I know they did what they did to make sure she received better hours and the days off she wanted. Felicia said if they offered me full-time it would come in the mail and I would have to accept it pretty quick. I'm not sure why when others had two weeks, I believe, to accept the offer. She also asked me about the PTO I had requested. I told her that we would not be going right now but that the system would not allow me to delete the PTO in ESS. She said she would just go in and disapprove it and that would work. She went into the department calendar. It was in the form of an Excel spreadsheet on her computer. I noticed that the supervisors' teams were color coded and that hers was green. The PTO time that I had requested (written down for Ethel a few days earlier) was in green. Felicia asked how to remove the green in the cell. I showed her how to access the "fill bucket" icon at the top of the screen. She seemed impressed and thanked me. She said that she was "computer illiterate."

I had my first Skymall order. It was for a 7-Star guest who purchased a cookware set for 22,600 RC's (Reward Credits). I had input some of the information but then went to get Felicia to show me how to complete it. We went into the Comp Screen and she showed me how to select the "Cascade" section. I did it quickly and she said I needed to put the information about the order in the Comment section, that is, the order number and a brief description. She went to another computer and reversed it. She then had me do it again. I then completed the order in Skymall using the Comp Receipt number. The guest wanted to know how much he had left in available cash, so I did the computation and told him he had $1800 available. He wanted the cash and Felicia reminded me that he could only get $500 which was the daily limit.

Although we can upgrade the account of a guest, who has Cherokee as their dominant property, from Gold to Platinum and Platinum to Diamond when their tier score meets or exceeds the required amount, I discovered that a guest does not automatically become a 7-Star just because their tier score reaches the required amount. The supervisor can put in the request with the guest's host (Sr. Account Executive Casino Host) and they make the determination, upgrade, and notification. I'm finally starting to see how these things are coming together and why they were not too happy that I wrote "Host Cash" for one of the 7-Star guests. Even though it was not a major infraction, I believe they felt I was infringing upon their territory. After all, I'm just a lowly TR Rep.

Saturday, July 20 – It's real busy in the casino. Not as many people gathering for the $150,000 free slot play giveaway as it was last time, but there was still a large number of entrants/participants. There were again, only 6 winners. I believe the promotion would do much better if the wealth were spread around. We get a lot of complaints from guests.

I had one guest who had been back 3 times to get a rewards card because every time she went to the promotions kiosk to swipe it, it said "Unable to process at this time." She thought it was something wrong with her card because I'd given her 3 more and she said it did the same thing. I checked with Linda to see if it was okay to go with the guest over to the kiosk to see if I could help, especially since the card had to be swiped between noon and 8pm and it was getting very close to 8pm. Linda said, "By all means, yes." I went over with the guest and sure enough we got the same response. I told the guest that I would go to another kiosk. I hurried over but was unable to get to the kiosk by the Main Cage in time. Linda told the guest we would take care of things and find a way to recompense her. Eventually, Linda gave me a handwritten non-cash voucher for $25 to take the guest. Since she was playing slots, it was easy to look up her location and find her. She was extremely grateful.

I talked briefly with Hilda and told her that she reminded me of someone. I told her that she was probably born either in September or November. She said she was born in September and asked me how I did that, that is, figure out her birth month. I told her because I taught school I because of the places I'd worked I usually ran into people with similar personalities and could usually pinpoint their birth month. Hilda was surprised when I shared with her that I had a BA, an MA, and a Ph.D. She asked me what I was doing there. I shared with her that my last job was at the Gila River Indian Community Juvenile Detention Center. I told her that I was making $54,000 a year. I told her briefly about my nonprofit organization and that it took us 8 years to get our first small grant. I told her about the Adult Education/GED grant we received from the Ariz. Dept. of Education and then the United Way grant. I told her that I could "see the devil coming." I told her that we lost our United Way grant. The better description was that we did not receive funding for the third year.

Felicia told me that she corrected the Skymall order we did the previous day because we didn't allow for the guest's discount. She said that next time I should complete the entire order and then use the calculation, which will include the discount, to deduct that amount from the Comp section. I thanked her and told her I would. Later that day, I went back into the screen to make sure I could find the right Comp area the next time. Since the orders are rare and few in between, it's easy for a TR rep to forget the process. However, I notice that there is an instruction document in the TR Rep folder that explains the process. I've decided that during slow days I would take time to read through every bit of the information in that folder.

My daughter said she was told that they thought she wanted day shift because of the time she filled in for another cage cashier who was on the day shift. She said they told her that her 4-10's and schedule would be back to normal next week.

Sunday, July 21 – Lance is the D/R on duty at the Rotunda. We did very well even though we had a line full of people. When there was a lull, Lance asked me how my daughter was doing. I told him that she was doing well. I did tell him that she had applied for the Table Games Dealer Training because she wanted to make more money. I told him that she likes to keep busy and that she doesn't like to just stand there with nothing to do. I told him that I told her that if they were going to pay her to just stand there, I told her to just stand there and collect her paycheck. Lance said that my daughter was very ambitious like her mother. I told him that I felt I was on my way out. He said that no, I had a lot more to do yet. I told him that I felt very old. He said that he didn't feel nearly as old as he was. I kept wondering to myself just how old he was, but wasn't about to ask him.

Linda came down from the TR in Earth Water to help us at one point. She was in uniform. Lance told us that we did a great job.

Chapter 19

Support Your Local Tribal Gaming Commission

It just occurred to me that most of the natives and/or tribal members in our department have Sunday off. I notice that most of the shops, stores, and of course, community agencies are closed on Sundays.

I had a Native American gentleman named Pilar in a suit and a long grey ponytail come sit by me. I was waiting on a guest when I noticed him there. Tilly and Lance were talking to him and Tilly was shaking his hand. I surmised that she was just meeting him for the first time. I heard him say that he was going to "hang out with Rachel for a while." I waited on the guest. He had an Iranian last name. He was asking about free tickets. I told him he would receive those in the mail. He was not pushy but kept asking me about them, so I told him I could check his account to see if we had the correct mailing address and if we had mailed anything to him. His address was correct and we had a couple of mailing scheduled for July 29th. I told him the last mailing to him was July 10th. I asked him if there was anything else I could help him with, and he said that was all. For some reason, because he kept looking at Pilar, I kept wondering if I was being spotlighted. It didn't matter because I try to be the same way with or without an audience. Pilar told me who he was. I noticed his badge said Gaming Commission. He asked me how long I'd been there and whether I liked working there. I told him yes, that it was fine. I wasn't about to tell him about what I'd gone through. The truth is I liked working there; I just didn't like how I was being treated with regard to upward movement. I waited on one Diamond guest and one first-time guest during the rest of the time Pilar was there. I believe he was there for both of them; however, I hadn't noticed when Pilar actually left. Both guests were very appreciative, especially since I always try to be lighthearted and tried to go the extra mile, if possible.

Lance asked me if I had "scared Pilar away." I told him, "I guess it was something I said." We were both being lighthearted. I told Lance that Pilar seemed like a nice guy.

Eunice was being real industrious like I was at one time at the Rotunda. She was emptying the trash cans and put an embosser cartridge and cleaning pad on our desks. She was never there when I used to do the cleaning of the desks and counters and the embossers. In fact, Linda, Morris, and I used to clean. I cleaned until Leslie, who used to be there during sunrise, told me she wanted to clean and do Combines so she had something to do, so I let her. I'm thinking that maybe I will want to get back to doing that. I'm not sure if Tilly, Barbara, Hilda, and Charles do the cleaning. I'm not there right now, so I don't know. While Eunice and I were walking back to be counted out, she talked about how she got full-time and Jack was giving her the days off and schedule she wanted. She asked me if I was full-time, and I told her no.

Lance counted me out and kept getting 51 for the total number of $5 coupon receipts and left over coupons. I told him there should only be 50. He told me to count them with him. I did, and we got 50. I said, "I told you." He smiled and said that I was very organized. I told him that "Linda taught me that." I usually write on the receipts the number of $5's, $20's, and $50's I used to redeem the coupon. This makes it much easier, Linda had told me, when the supervisor had to count out the Rep's money. She was right.

Linda showed me the TR board in the Buzz area. I had a positive written comment from one of the guests. Looks like the email had been sent to Felicia. There was also one for Carol and Leslie also.

Chapter 20

Cherokee People, not Cherokee Employee

Monday, July 22 - During Buzz they were talking about an incident where they found a body in the river the night before. One of the reps, Mona, said it was a 38-year old woman. Later, someone else said it was an 84-year old man. I told them in Buzz that Helen had told us that at least one person dies each month at the casino or the Cherokee area. She's right. There has been at least one every month that I've been there.

I had gone to HR to pick up a transfer form because I intended to apply for the internal position: Cherokee Leader Associate. Lester was there. I got the form and left. I then went back and asked him about the VIP Host position. He said it was closed. I asked him how we would know when a position closes because there was no date listed on the posting outside the HR area just across from Security. He said the internal positions are listed in Keyweb (the company intranet) and that the closing dates are there. He said the position is offered internally from Friday to Thursday and then it goes External. He said the External positions are posted until filled. I told him I had applied for the VIP Host position; it was apparent from his manner that his manager and/or other staff had already talked about me. He was not too friendly – in fact, haughty almost. He said that the departments can choose who they want to interview and would not interview a candidate if they did not think they were "a good fit for the department." I felt a pit in my stomach. The depression came back but I had to muster through it.

It was pretty much a slow day as usual. Lance was D/R on duty. I had a guest who was a brand new guest. I was still a bit distracted by my disappointment. She plainly asked for the "Buy One, Get One Free Buffet," however, I clicked on the $5 Free Slot Play. I realized my error. I figured if I swiped another card I could still give her the buffet, which is what I did. The guest's whose card I swiped was not due any free gift. This was a definite no-no. However, I gave the guest the buffet coupon, not realizing the guest's name and TR # would be on the coupon and they would have to show ID for it. Lance answered the phone from Linda who asked me to call her. She said the guest was at Chef's Stage and had a coupon that had someone else's name on it. I told Gene about my mistake and she told me it was easier to correct. She made sure that the other guest was not due anything and that I didn't have hidden jackpot coupon or anything like that. She told me to do a handwritten voucher and take it to the guest at Chef's Stage. Had I not been distracted and thinking a bit more clearly, I would have done that instead. I then remembered that we had to do handwritten vouchers in the past. I was not feeling too great about myself. I really needed someone to talk to. When I went up to Chef's Stage, the manager gave me the incorrect coupon and I had the guest sign the correct handwritten one. I apologized to the guest. The guest was very understanding. While coming from Chef Stage, I saw my daughter and briefly told her about my encounter with Lester in HR. She told me I needed to sue Caesar's and document how I felt about what I went through. I told her that you can't sue the tribe. She reminded me that the tribe owned the casino, but it was managed by Harrah's and Caesars.

Carrie was talking to Victoria about her new position and boasted that she would be starting next Friday. I felt even worse because I knew that as tribal members, they could get just about any position they wanted to get. I kept thinking how Lester said the department could determine that you were not a good fit and just not interview you. I kept thinking how they could tell that Natasha, who also worked in Total Rewards and was 5 months pregnant and did not have the best handle on the English language, was a good fit, yet I, who also worked in Total Rewards (albeit not as long as Natasha and not a D/R Supervisor), but more education, supervisory experience, and additional skills and background, was not a good fit. Once again, it comes down to a combination of my age and being a black woman. I then realized that the VIP Host position is in the same department (Casino Marketing) as the Sr. Account Executive Casino Host for which I already applied. Even though they already interviewed me, I had not heard anything but did see that the position was reposted on July 12. I realized then that they did not want me for the position, even though they had 9 to fill. Also, Lester had said the Sr. Account Exec. Casino Host position was still available. My being a black woman and my age are the only variables I can find in the whole scenario. There are none in that department. I truly feel something is amiss and not on the "up and up" in that department. Whatever it is, it's to my detriment.

Cynthia and Tilly came down from the Earth Water TR area. Even though they did stand for guests, there were times when Cynthia (7-Star chair), Victoria (Diamond chair) and Tilly in the 3rd seat did not stand because they were talking with Muriel who was standing in between Cynthia and Victoria. I don't fault them because it had been a long day and week for everyone. We all get tired. I was quiet most of the day and so was Barbara. Barbara was very tired. I was more depressed than tired. Even so, I maintained my UPA (Upbeat Positive Attitude) with the guests. Muriel came over and said hello. She commented on the weather to get me talking a bit. She asked about my daughter's hours. I told her a bit about how they were changed. I explained that it was just miscommunication on the part of my daughter's two managers, Wayland and Randy. She said that Randy was a nice guy. I told her I thought he was also. I shared with her about my daughter's "interview" for the Table Games Dealer Training and the outcome. I told her that my daughter was pretty upset. I shared with her that I told my daughter that some things are a "blessing in disguise." Muriel agreed and said that also "The grass is not always greener." I said I told my daughter that she works in a good department because they made her full-time after the first two weeks she was there and how they usually let her have the hours she asks for. I said that I usually just ask, seek, and knock and let God open and close the doors accordingly. I said that I know things will get better. Muriel agreed, and then said, "At least that's what I keep telling myself." We both just gave a briefly laugh of relief. I know that she had been passed over by Ivan and Jack for the D/R Supervisor position initially when she applied from the Finance Dept. I was told that she had gone to Ivan and Jack and "read them the riot act." I guess she was pretty angry and dismayed.   still haven't figured out if Natasha is a tribal member for sure, but I don't believe she is. I know that Muriel has been passed over for the regular Supervisor position when Felicia got the job. However, I know that they "threw" Muriel a "bone" when they certified her as an interviewer. I know that in Muriel's case it is a definite case of age discrimination, along with the fact that I've been told you can't really complain or comment on anything there. They just want you to smile as though everything is all right all of the time. This is fine when you're with a guest; however, you should be able to let your supervisor, manager, and staff know when something is not quite right. It's a classic case of "the emperor is not wearing any clothes." Everyone sees the nakedness and knows it, but no one is supposed to mention it.

Linda counted Cynthia's coupons and she was one over. She's supposed to get a write-up; I wonder if she will. Victoria was supposed to be counted out next, but she said Linda could count mine because she said, "It's Rachel's Friday" meaning I would be off for the next two days. It was gracious of her, but I also know that she didn't want to leave and just have Linda and I there. She knows I talk with Linda at times and that she talks about Linda at times. I had zero variance.

Chapter 21

Atlanta Poker Club Blues

July 23 – Sara and I drove to Atlanta to play with Interstate Poker Club and to get lobster at Red Lobster in Decatur. It was one of the few times that I didn't get out within the first 15-20 minutes of play. I really don't like NL Hold'em or NL anything. Some people like that gambling component of it where all you have is riding on that one hand. I really don't like this and it doesn't give me a thrill at all. All I really wanted to do was just play cards with a group of people. If we could play with just the chips for free and win nothing at all; this would suit me just fine. However, all those people want to win the $100 and the tournament to get higher points for a chance to be entered into the monthly tournament. At their monthly tournament you can win $3,000. So, it's worth it in the long run. They are a yellow venue which means players can buy chips up to three times. I had comp tickets from when we played two weeks prior where I won $30 worth on the video slot games. You can't win cash but you can win bar cash, they call it. We bought the fish and chips and they were surprisingly very good. They came with hush puppies that were brown and crisp, instead of mushy like some other places where we've had them. Two different hands I was bluffed out where I would have won, but the Black guy "bullied" me. Another hand I had K-Q and I won a good pot because I had the King on the flop; however, the turn gave the same bully guy two pair. On the river, I had the nut straight. I played it cool and was able to get them to call. However, on one hand I had pocket Queens. Another lady had pocket 8's. She ended up winning because the flop had two 9's, a 7 and a 7. The two 9's slowed me down and I didn't bet it. I've been beaten so many times when I thought I had the best hand and didn't. However, I checked it and apparently she caught up. The 6 came on the river and she beat me with a straight. My daughter had already gotten out. When we were down to 2 tables I was already to leave. By then, they had turned on the loud music and it was darker in there. It seems Vince, the Tournament Director, likes that type of atmosphere. I really don't. So, I went all with my K-J suited hand. I was called by the same bully guy who had A-9 off-suite. There was no pair for either of us so he beat me with just Ace high. He put his palm out graciously however when he beat me and smiled. We went for the lobster. I usually get the lobster and Sara will get something else somewhere else. I just love the butter sauce and the bread is so good. I believe their Red Lobster is the best that I've had and I've eaten at several Red Lobsters in Atlanta, Georgia, the one in Sevierville, Tennessee, the one in Mesa, Arizona, and the one in Gilbert, Arizona. Oh, how I wish they would replace Paula Deen's at Cherokee with a Red Lobster! However, I don't know if they would be as good a cook as the Decatur chef. So far, I haven't found very good food in North Carolina, especially within Cherokee, Sylva, or Whittier. I recommend Brio's to everyone. However, just like every place we go, we have to come home and cook it some more and add olive oil and a bit more seasoning to it. Then, it's really good and edible!

July 24 – Today was the giveaway for the '57 Buick, worth over $70,000. I would find out later that the winner took the car instead of the cash which is only $35,000. It's really a Catch-22 because either way the winner has to pay taxes. If they take the car, they have to come up with the tax money eventually; however, if they take the cash, they will have the money upfront to pay the taxes. At least, I believe this is how it works for when one wins a car valued at such a large amount (over $11,000). The most that I've ever won is $5,000 which was a bad beat in a poker cash game. I asked for a check and deposited the check quickly. I was afraid to spend any of it because I knew it would just go right through my hands ("easy come, easy go"), and that's just what happened. Even though we look at it as "easy come, easy go" because it's free, most of our guests would not agree that it was really "free" because they have expended monies in either the slots, poker, and/or table games to win entries into the drawing. The more you play, the more entries you acquire, and hence, based on statistics, the higher the probability that your name will be chosen from among the thousands in the barrel. Sometimes, based on a guest's play, they are granted bonus entries from Promotions which are sent to the guest via postal mail and/or email.

It's my day off, so I decided to make some calls to follow-up on my interview and position applications. I called around 10am and left a message for Olga to ask her about the VIP Host position because she had told me she would cross out the Sr. Acct. Exec. Casino Host position and put "VIP Host" on the "position applying for" line. Because they are doing cross-training in HR, Olga was upstairs doing New Hire and Helen was working with applicants in the downstairs HR area. When Olga answered the phone, she said "Yeah," in a short tone. I was surprised to hear someone answer the phone that way, especially in HR. I was taken aback. I wasn't sure if she knew it was an outside call and/or if she had a trying day. I do realize that it's not an easy job. She seemed frustrated talking to me because I wanted to know why I was not chosen to be interviewed for the VIP Host position. She said, "We keep trying to tell you!" I said, "We?" I realized that they had been having conversations about me, more than likely after I had talked to Penny, the manager in HR. Olga told me that if an "01" is found, my application is not even sent over. I also found out from her that an "01" can be recruited for an external position and supersede a current employee. She also said that HR does not determine who gets interviewed, that applications from applicants meeting the minimum requirements are sent to the hiring manager, and that it is the hiring manager who determines who gets interviewed. I told her I was also expecting to see what was written on my application as to why I was not interviewed and/or offered the position. She said that no one, expect HR, sees what is written on the applications. She said that if I wanted an answer as to why I was not interviewed and/or offered a position, I would have to talk to the hiring managers. She gave me Delilah's name for the Sr. Acct. Exec. Casino Host position (which I already had) and Bertha's name for the VIP Host position.

I called Delilah and received her voice mail, so I left a message for her. I told her that I was following up on the position for which I applied and wanted to briefly discuss something with her. I did not hear back from her, so I called Erma. After identifying myself I told her I was just trying to find out why I was not selected for an interview for the VIP Host position. She said that she did not know who I was. I asked if she had seen my application and she told me that she had not. I told her that HR said they had sent my application over and that I was an internal applicant. She said that it is HR who sends over the applicants to be interviewed. Erma said that the manager just interviews who is sent to them.

By now I realize that someone is not telling me the truth because I am getting conflicting stories. More investigation will reveal what is actually going on.

I called Phoebe in HR. I told her I was not trying to bug her but just wanted to follow up on the Special Events & Promotions Supervisor position. She seemed more settled and patient than did Olga. Phoebe said that she had been on vacation. I told her that they had told me she was on vacation and would work on the placement when she returned. I informed her that I had taken Superlap. She said she did see that. She told me to hold on a second and she would look through my file and at my application. She told me that the hiring manager had extended an offer to an external applicant but the applicant declined the offer. I realized at that point that they hadn't even bothered to interview me because the last I heard from Olga, who was previously handling the position, was that they had not started interviews yet. Phoebe said that she would talk with the hiring manager and find out if they wanted to interview me. She told me to check back with her on Monday and that she would be there until 5 pm. I thanked her for her help and hung up.

I called Arnette and she told me that she didn't want a full-time position, but that Jack had offered it to her and she was going to take it for two reasons. She said he had told her that because of Obamacare she would need the medical insurance and that she felt being full-time would make her look good when she transferred out, which was the next step in her plans. She said Jack told her that the 11pm to 7:30am slots were already filled. I told her how I was tired of how I seemed to be undermined as a Black woman everywhere I go. She said, "Well, all right, Sister, if you're tired of it, do something about it! You don't ask them for what you want, you ask God for what you want!" We both claimed a full-time position for me and the hours that I wanted.

There seems to be a foreboding of something evil coming and I could feel a dark spirit. I wasn't sure of what it was. The printer connected to the computer kept restarting itself for no reason at all. It had never done that before. I started to rebuke the devil and his forces and prayed. My daughter stated doing the same thing. We started praising God. My daughter told me later that one of the neighbors said that she was experiencing some strange things like that and that she felt it was the spirit of the neighbor in Unit #3 who had committed suicide. It's so strange because I remember when she came over our house the one time how she kept staring at our microwave on top of the refrigerator and the two printers on top of the island in the kitchen. The neighbor in Unit #1 eventually moved out a few days later. I wasn't sure if it was because she had experienced some of the same eerie things, or because the landlord finally came down on her because she had both a cat and a dog and no pets were allowed, or because she found a better place to live. She never talked to me, so I had no idea what her reasons were. Since she'd never said hello, of course she didn't bother to say goodbye. Go figure.

Chapter 22

Really Hidden Jackpots

July 25 – Today is my 6-hour day from 12pm to 6pm, as Jack as scheduled me for the last 3 weeks. Sara is working from 11am to 7pm, so I'll drop her off and then come home and get washed up and dressed. I notice how much different it is during the morning hours, especially in the summer. I like the climate, both that of the weather and that of the people. I had a great time at work. I had prayed and read my word, so I was ready with my whole armor. It seemed as if the Hidden Jackpot was still a hit with the guests. Many of them would have a look on their faces like, "Ok, yeah, here's another thing that I won't win – same old, same old . . ." Here was my spiel:

"We have a promotion going on called Hidden Jackpot. From noon until 8pm you can swipe your card daily at one of our eight kiosks up until August 25th. If a ticket prints out, you've won between 5 and 500 dollars in free slot play. If no ticket prints out, then you've won bonus entries into the August 25th drawing. After the August 2th grand prize giveaway, they're going to give away one million dollars at every one of our properties."

When people heard this, the first thing they ask anxiously is: "Where do I swipe it?" If I'm down in the Rotunda, I tell them that the nearest one is just on the other side of the Directory, but I also let them know there is one on the 2nd Floor, up the escalators, next to the Chef Stage Buffet, and there is one just to the right of the Main Cage Cashier on the first floor. If I'm on the 2nd Floor TR in Earth Water, like I was today, I told them to use the one just to the right of us. However, I was told by a couple of staff members that the kiosk was not working, so I was sending guests to the Chef Stage Buffet kiosk and downstairs to the Main Cage Cashier kiosk. I told a few guests how I seemed to be lucky for other people but not for myself. All of the guests happened to be of European-descent. I had high energy because I am normally a morning to mid-morning person and this is when I'm at my best. However, I am still good with the guests no matter what time of day it is. I told the guests my story about how I was not an employee of Casino Arizona, but had been a guest. I was sitting next to (actually two seats over with an empty seat between us) a guest who was playing the Wheel of Fortune slot machine. They were the 25 cents machines, which I believe are still 25 cents in most casinos. I know Cherokee's is still 25 cents. I told the guest that I was lucky for other people but not for me and that she would probably win because I was sitting next to her. Sure enough, she was playing the maximum because she could afford it, and she won $452,000. They were taking her picture with a huge check with the amount printed on it. She was happy but seemed controlled in her joy. It did not seem as though she had never had that much money in her life. I, like so many other people, have never had that much money at one time – ever, and it doesn't seem like it will ever happen. I was happy for her but it was colored by the question: "Why wasn't that me?" Of course, I never shared the latter parts of this story with the Cherokee guests. For some reason, they kept coming back, having won something. One person won $500 free slot play, one person one $100 in free slot play, and another had just received a new player's card from me and came back to show me her TITO (Time-In Time-Out) Ticket from the slot machine. She had won $1,006. She gave me a "High Five." I was so happy for them. This was a big change from when I was a guest. I was so envious of them. Now, I am so happy when they win. I realize how hard it is when you gamble and take chances. I realize you can be up one day and down the next. I realize that casinos were not designed for you to win. They were designed to "bleed you slowly financially," so to speak, but show you a good time and have you enjoy what you're doing at the same time. In other words, the casino is there to entertain you. It's quite ingenious when you think about it. They are adept at marketing their products and services. You get offers for free hotel stay, free meals, free slot play, free complimentary drinks when you play, and sometimes, based on your tier level, free tickets to concerts and events. They are tops in the hospitality and entertainment industry. However, there is a dark side that only staff members and guests who are not highly revered because of their low C.A.P. scores know. C.A.P. is something we're told that we're never to tell guests about, although some guests have found out about this from their Representatives and/or VIP Host. It is the calculation the casino uses to determine how much you play. It is used in their decisions to provide you with a personal guest representative or not. If you are a player with a high C.A.P. you are bound to receive a great deal of amenities. Even having said this, there seems to be some discrepancies among amenities given to Black women who are Diamond players and non-Black women Diamond players. One Black female guest told me that she was very concerned because other guests were receiving $100 and higher free slot play where she received only $30 and $60 in free slot play in the mail. Her C.A.P. was over 1700. She had asked to speak to her representative. Muriel had come over to where I was that day when the guest was telling me about her situation. Muriel said that she would have to send her rep an email because there was no way that the guest would be able to contact her. I should have followed up, but I did not at the time. I have not seen the guest back at Cherokee since that day.

I noticed that none of the reps were eating candy or chewing gum and seemed a bit sullen. I wasn't sure if someone had said I told Ethel about what they had been doing. I didn't tell Ethel, of course, but Victoria had. I kept wondering if Victoria had made it seem as though I told on them. I asked Beverly how life was treating her because she looked a bit down. She said she was single again. I asked her if she was happy about it and she said she was. I told her that God has a better plan for her and that he was someone better in store for her. I then told her and Lena about how someone asked me about my children after my divorce. I said I told them, "I have two children; I used to have a third child but I divorced him."

Chapter 23

And You Shall Receive

I noticed that Nicholas, one of the DR Supervisors, was upstairs and was in uniform. That was the first time I'd ever seen him in uniform. I then realized that most of the non-tribal members in TR were older. It seems that they either didn't have degrees and/or just worked there because of the great benefits.

I asked Jack, that morning when he was giving my money, whether I would be getting a full-time position. He looked at me surprised and said, "Yeah, if you want it." He said, "No one has talked to you yet?" I told him no. I said this because Felicia had said Jack would get with me. It was just at the time Carol was coming in the door. I didn't know if she was getting counted out, counted in, or going on break. I asked Jack if he knew what the hours would be. He said that there were so set hours. Both he and Carol started saying that the only people who have the same hours each day are the ones who open and the ones who close. He must have been referring to the Earth Water TR because the Rotunda is open 24 hours a day; however, he may have been referring to our casino day: 6am to 5:59 am.

When I got home I had a voice mail on my phone that Ivan had returned my call from the week prior. It was my guess that Jack had talked to him about what I had asked. Also, Delilah and/or Bertha may have told him I had called. I was a bit tired and not sure if I wanted to call him back. I didn't know if he was planning to scold me for calling HR or what the conversation would be.

July 26 – It took a great deal of prayer and studying my word. I called Ivan back that morning. I congratulated him on winning the Q2 Leadership Award. I told him that I wasn't sure what it was. He said it was one of those things where he looks good because his staff made him look good. He said he really should be thanking us. I told him, well, good job. I asked him if I would be getting a full-time position. He said that most definitely I would be one of them. He said that when we had the meeting a while back, he felt that there would be more openings but he couldn't promise because sometimes, as a manger, your plans don't always come to pass. He said that Felicia will be getting with me that evening. He said that if she doesn't mention it, to call him back. He also said that not everybody would be offered the full-time, so I should just keep it low-key out of respect for the feelings of others. I hadn't planned on shouting it from the rooftops because it was only a minor victory. He asked me if there was anything else. I told him that was all. He said, "We're good?" I said yes and thanked him for returning my call. I had decided to choose my battles wisely, so I didn't press the issue about the matrix because he was at least giving me the full-time position. How and what it plays out to be remains to be seen. I still brooded a bit because I know I should have been full-time before 5 other people. I should be used to this kind of treatment by now. I know my ancestors were. We were always fighting for the basics when we should have had a lot more. In other words, everyone was enjoying a large slice of the pie while were first unaware that the bakery even existed. When we discovered the bakery existed, others were being taught how to make their own pies. While we were legally denied entrance into the bakery, others were setting up their own bakeries. While we were fighting for our right to enter the bakery, others were already hiring other people in their bakeries. While we were fighting for our right to work for the bakery, others were offering us the right to a few of the crumbs of their pies. Only God can right the terrible wrong that has been done to us – man never will.

Lance is the DR on duty and told us there would be changes made to policy. He was reading a few of the changes from the WINET newsletter. However, none of us saw any changes. It was more of a reminder of what our appearance should be and how we should abstain from wearing certain size plugs in the ears, certain size earrings, maintaining the dress code, when and when not to wear our badges when off-duty, and not entering the EDR or backhouse except with permission. I wasn't sure specifically because there seemed to be some conflict as to what we were told in New Hire and the policy, but I signed the acknowledgement anyway and would ask questions when the situation arose and I wasn't sure. There was another sheet on the counter where several employees had signed and there were different policy changes. I didn't sign yet because I wanted a copy to go home and read it first. There was some writing on the Buzz board that Lance went over. It was emphasized that standing up to greet guests and acknowledging guests in line were initiatives and that we should adhere to them and should not have to be coached.

Arnette was down in the Rotunda for about 20 minutes or so. I was down at the end and she anxiously wanted to find out if God had answered prayer. I nodded my head but I was trying to tell her that Ivan wanted me not to say anything. She squealed with excitement and said congratulations. I turned to see Victoria staring down at us. The next thing I knew Victoria came over and put her hands on my shoulders and said, "I hear congratulations are in order." I looked at her quizzically because my mind was racing because for a moment I wasn't sure to what she was referring. I searched my memory banks and remembered that only Jack and Carol knew I had asked about the full-time, but I wasn't sure if she was referring to the positions for which I had applied. After a moment, I whispered, "full-time?" and she nodded. I said "yes." She said good job. She said she had seen we had some openings for TR Rep positions and she said she told Jack that she hoped they had offered the positions to internal candidates first. She said he had told her, "We did." I told her, "Great looking out." Arnette was called to get counted out for the day. The next thing I knew Brad was congratulating me and then proceeded to look at the schedule and started talking about who remained part time still. He said Cynthia can't get full-time. I didn't know why. I had heard that Leslie would not receive full-time because she had too many points. Brad also said that Jeffrey was trying to transfer out and didn't want full-time. I'm not sure if Alice wanted full-time or not. Charles had said he was too new and wouldn't get full-time yet. However, apparently newness seems to have nothing to do with it. I knew that Sean and Barbara were over-the-top and always recommended everything to the guest that was going on that day. There were very personable and knowledgeable. However, Beverly was never over-the-top and Hilda was still struggling with learning everything. I know that the bottom line was I was an "uppity little Black gal" at first, or so it seemed to others. It seems I was judged by what I looked like rather than what I accomplished and of what I was capable.

Victoria showed me that she, Leslie, and I had been listed in the Service Stars section of the Cherokee casino news. Ivan had his picture with someone else and had received the Q2 Leadership Award for the Transportation (Valet) and Total Rewards. How ironic I thought at first because of what had happened to me; however, after receiving the award, he seemed to more so exemplify this quality. Perception is a strange thing.

Chapter 24

Breaker, Breaker, Copy That

I had been in the 7-Star chair for a while when Brad came up behind me and told me he was relieving me and that I could go on my 30 minute break because I had signed up for 10 o'clock. I thought he had already checked with Linda or Linda had told him to tell me. So I left. When I got back, Victoria and Linda were just coming out of Linda's office and Victoria said something about "Rachel's back." A few minutes later, Linda asked me to let her know when I leave. I told her that I thought she told them to tell me I could leave. She asked me who it was and for the moment I didn't remember it was Brad. I told her it was Victoria. When I went back inside to sit at the 4th seat, I saw Brad in the 7-Star chair and I remembered. I wanted to hurry back and tell Linda of mistake but a guest had come up. I was waiting on the guest, but asked if they would excuse for a moment like I do when I have to print a picture on a 7-Star card or get a pamphlet. However, Felicia came in and I told her I needed to tell Linda something real quickly. She said, "I'm here, what do you need?" I told her it was something I needed to make sure Linda knew. She told me to finish taking care of the guest first. So, I did and went and told Linda it was Brad, and not Victoria. She said, "Oh – that makes more sense." She said later that she told Ethel about it and she said that Brad thinks he's in charge "down there" (meaning the Rotunda). I remembered the conversation Brad and Linda had one time when he didn't think it was necessary to check with a supervisor before going on break because we were "all adults." After that time, I was told by Carol and another rep on two different times that Felicia said I could go on break. However, I made sure that I checked with Felicia before going.

I noticed that Felicia never intentionally sits me in the 7-Star chair but she will sit Beverly in that seat. I notice that she won't intentionally set me in the Diamond chair, but she will sit Barbara in that seat. These are just observations. I believe Felicia has my best interest at heart. In fact, she did spotlights on me so I could have more favorable input in my file. I appreciate her for that.

July 27 – Edward was still in the Buzz area when I came in at 4pm. There were quite a lot of us in there. He counted out our money to us. Ethel talked about the 7-Star cash giveaway and the shopping spree. She reminded us about the "stand and greet" initiative and warned us that no one should have to be coached. In other words, we would get a 3-count write-up to being booted out the door. Poindexter kept making half-jokes about his "stash" and Ethel said that he could eat but not when out in front of the guests. Poindexter also congratulated me on getting my name in the paper. I flipped my hair like Zelda had done about a week prior.

It was fairly busy at the Rotunda TR. It was business as usual. There seems to be a whole different crop of people who come in during the evening and late night and who come down to the Rotunda than those who go to the Earth Water TR and come in during the earlier hours. The Hidden Jackpot is only until 8pm, so a lot of them miss it and we end up promoting the restaurants until 11pm and telling them the Food Court is open 24 hours. Some of them tell them about the Essence Lounge, the Music Walk Series, and the Hidden Jackpot for the following day. We got extremely busy at one point, mostly around 7pm. During lunch, I didn't eat. I slept for 15 minutes and spent about 10 minutes in the massage chair. I always notice two overweight people who lay down on the L-shaped couch head-to-head with both of them having their cell phones lifted just above their heads. It appears they are playing some time of app game. A few people come in the

Quiet Room to sleep, rest, read, and others use the computers through the doors.

Around 11 pm I was sitting in the Diamond chair talking to Lance who is in uniform and sitting in the 7-Star Chair. He said that others tell him that he doesn't like to take breaks. He said when he finds a good chair he doesn't like to let go of it because the other computers don't work as well. Around that time, a guest came up to get a replacement player's card and he told me that he'd been away for a while because he just had a brain operation. I could see what appeared to be a scar across the upper part of his brow (frontal lobe). I didn't comment on it but just went through my pleasantries as usual. When he left, Lance said he never knows what to say when someone tells you they've just had a brain operation. I told him it's probably best not to say anything, especially when you don't really know what part of his brain has been operated on. Lance laughed. It's strange how my daughter used to always say he reminded her of an avatar when he wore his glasses.

I liked Lance. He was friendly and you usually have good conversation with him. He had a calming nature. I remember him giving me a ride home one evening because my daughter had inadvertently taken both cell phones and I couldn't get in touch with her. I believe this was before we had Internet and the Magic Jack number was reachable. I didn't even know where the service elevator was but Lance went this route to get to where his truck was parked on the 4th Floor, I believe. He was reluctant at first to give me a ride. I could see it on his face. I think part of the fact is that he's married. However, I asked him which way he went home and he said the 441. He knew he couldn't get out of it because he was going right by where I live. A few weeks prior, he'd heard from someone that I lived at the Mountain Peak Apartments. Apparently, Lance knew the owner of the apartments. He said the man owned a great deal of property and was a self-made entrepreneur who had quite a bit of money. He said you'd never know it by the way he dresses, but he was pretty well off.

Felicia counted us out that evening. I had zero-variance. Felicia baked a cake and brought it in. It was extremely delicious. She told us what kind it was, but it didn't register. My mind was elsewhere. She said she loves to bake but she can't eat it. I'm not sure if this is because she's a diabetic or because she's on a diet.

Chapter 25

A Few Good Things

July 28 – It's so odd having to work on a Sunday. However, it's even odder having to work on Saturday. This is the first job I've had where I had to wear a uniform, punch a time clock, and work on weekends. I remember Muriel telling me that it was the same with her. It's an interesting industry to work in. The casino has its pros and cons. It's one of the few places that is open 24 hours a day and never closes. You can be homeless and, if you're strategic, can almost live at the casino. As long as you're not drunk, on drugs, and hostile, but simply mind your own business, you're pretty much left alone. You would have to keep moving around and at least play a little bit on the slots and/or table games. You would do best if you at least had a car to sleep in, however. My daughter and I were in transition when we were first hired. We had applied for several positions at Cherokee when we lived in Atlanta. Several months had gone by with no response. My daughter was receiving her check from attending school and I had bits and pieces of income from the home-based business. However, she was unable to finish the last semester of classes and had a small bit of income from the few hours they gave her at Taco Bell, and our water bill was over $800. We did find out that someone had been using our water, which is why the bill was so high. Of course, the bill was over several months.

My daughter always believes she can take a few hundred dollars and turn it into a lot more. Unfortunately, we never do that, and if we do, we end up giving it back, as most gamblers do, and instead, end up handing over more of hard-earned or hard-won funds back to the casino. My daughter has won playing poker online. From experience, I tried to get her to cash it out. On two different occasions she has $300 and $700, respectively. Because the online casinos make the withdrawal process so complicated with a long wait period for your check to arrive, you end up playing back (that is losing) what you win. We would later realize that online casinos are the worst. Never trust anything electronic because it can be manipulated ever so easily. We also realized that sometimes what you think is a person against whom you're playing, is really a computer or several computers. One of our poker friends, Raul, in the APC (Atlanta Poker Club) had previously told us that the online poker games are based on algorithms. In fact, they create bad beats on purpose to elicit action. This gets the players to invest more money in pots. Since the poker games, Hold'em, Omaha, Stud, and Razz are based on decisions to bet, call, raise, or fold after each card play, a computer can be programmed to make sure players start with relatively good odds of winning at specific points in the game play, that is, enough to place additional bets. This drives up the amount of the pot, thereby increasing the "take" of the house (online casino). Stock markets and investments work pretty much the same way. However, with stock markets, events are the driving forces that cause investors to buy or sell a specific stock, mutual fund, or bond. Either way, the brokers (the house) always get their cut (take).

My daughter and I both were at Cherokee Casino because Promotions sent me an email that I had reached Platinum status and offered me a few days of free hotel stay and sent me a few $5 and $10 free slot play. Since we were there on a Monday, we decided to go to HR and check on our applications we'd submitted months ago. We'd done this almost 6 months prior but we were trying to get my daughter hired, not me. It had never really ever occurred to me to work for the casino. When I look back on it, if I had to work there, I wish I'd started there when I was younger. My daughter had tried repetitively to get a job at the casino when she was younger, but to no avail. During the 6-month prior period, my daughter had taken the Math Test and she, like me, when I would take it the second time we were there when I was trying to get a job there, thought the plus (+) signs on the page were division (÷) symbols. This is one of the reasons they were offering her a temporary housekeeping position, we reasoned. However, the person who was supposed to call my daughter never called her. It was not until the second time around when we went to HR while on a complimentary hotel stay for 3 days that I realized what I thought to be division symbols were really plus symbols. I discovered this because the intake person, who I later discovered was named Sara also, told me I had a low score on the Math Test. I told her that can't be because I was a high school teacher and taught Math. That's when I realized and asked her about the symbols. She confirmed that they were plus symbols and not division symbols. She allowed me to retake the test. Apparently I did well because they offered me the TR Rep position. My daughter did exceptionally well because she finished the entire test. They offered her the Cage Cashier, which is surprising, because it paid less. I would later discover, after talking with Beverly, that she did not do as well on the Math and that she had applied for the Cage Cashier; however, they offered her the TR Rep position. The fact that she is tribal member explains it.

We had not anticipated interviewing for the positions the next day. It would be too hard to drive back to Atlanta; also, we already had rooms for the next 2 days. I agreed to an interview with Ethel for the next day. I told them that I don't normally interview in jeans; however, I explained my situation. The interview was not too grueling. The last question was an interesting one. However, she said she has been trying to get rid of that question. She gave me a small square object and told me that I could decide what I wanted it to be, but she wanted me to sell it to her. I don't remember everything I said, but she was very impressed and told me it was the best she'd seen yet. She said that she had reservations about how far away we lived. I told her that we would transition and eventually move to North Carolina. In my mind, you go where the job is. My ex-business partner and ex-fiancée (supposedly) told me that it was silly to move to another state for a part-time job. However, I considered the source. He had disappointed me in so many respects that I wasn't about listen to anything he had to say on any subject. Ethel gave me the walk-around through the casino to view the TR areas. She showed me the Motor Coach area and I met a few people that I would not remember. We went upstairs to the Earth Water TR area and I met people I would not remember. We then went down to the Rotunda TR area and I met people I would not remember. It's interesting, because the only person I met that I would remember during that time was Ivan, the TR Manager. This is because he was a tall, big man. I would learn later that he and Ethel were tribal members.

Chapter 26

Employee Depreciation

On shift down at the Rotunda was Eunice, Lena, Victoria, Jeffrey, Leslie, Hilda, Charles, and Linda. Some of them were earlier shift staff and would leave between 5pm and 7pm. Lance was the DR on duty that day. Leslie was quiet when it was just a few of us there. I told her welcome back and asked how she was feeling. She said she was better. I told her I had been concerned because her friend had told us she was in the hospital. I told her that some people don't make it through situations like that. She said she considered herself very lucky. I knew that the Lord had allowed her to go through that situation to humble her and hopefully, get her to understand that you cannot treat a child of the Most High God just any kind of way. However, he tells us to never be glad at their calamity. I was truly glad she was all right. It didn't matter what she'd said about me or how she and Esmerelda had talked about me. Esmerelda is the one who told me where Veteran's Park was, the place where they were holding the Employee Appreciation event on August 5 and August 6. We had to sign up in our department for one day or the other. I notice that Brad, Ivan, Beverly, Jack, and a few others had signed up for Monday. Obviously, I couldn't sign up for Monday because I worked on Mondays.

I overheard Eunice ask Esmerelda something that had to do with someone she was waiting for who would return by August 22nd. Eunice said, "It's almost here." Esmerelda was saying yes in a low voice. She wasn't looking my way, as if she really didn't want me to know what was going on. I asked if she was getting married on August 22nd. She said, "No, not yet." She just said he was taking care of some business. It was my daughter who wisely said later that she thought he must be in jail for drugs or something. Since they never tell me anything, I really didn't know. It seems you tell one person anything and everybody in that department knows about it. I make sure I don't tell ANYONE anything that I don't mind if it gets out to someone else.

I noticed that Victoria was acting a bit different. It could have been that she was just tired but her manner was different towards me than it was when Leslie was not there. That's when I sensed that there had been conversations about me. I know that Eunice talks about me because she talks a great deal about things and other people, not necessarily in a negative way, but just about them. Victoria and Leslie both do the same thing. One unsettling episode was when Victoria told me before Charles and Hilda got there, that the way she used to do the sitting of reps was by shifting to the left. She said that she thought we should go back to that. When Eunice had gone on break, I sat in the 7-Star chair where she had been sitting, only because Victoria, Charles, and Hilda were waiting on guests at their counters. When the guests were gone, I asked Victoria if she wanted to tell Charles and Hilda what she told me. She tried to say it in a non-harsh manner, but she told me "Shut up and sit down." She meant for me to go ahead and just sit in the 7-Star chair, because I had started to just move down. However, the words threw me for a loop.

Victoria was being counted out an hour early. When she left, I told Hilda that things were really strange and that I wasn't sure what was going on. I told her that I didn't like it when people were not the same and consistent to me. I told her that I would figure it out. I tried to get Hilda to go and sit in the Diamond chair and both she and Hilda said that I should be there because I had seniority and had been there longer. I told them that there was no seniority and that length of time there obviously had no bearing; otherwise, I would have been appointed to full-time before a whole lot of other people. I wasn't trying to make her feel bad, but I noticed she did cast her eyes down and she was sort of quiet. I believe this is why she may have said something to Lance later when I tried to help her with two guests who'd come to her window a bit intoxicated. I keep forgetting that she worked in the prison system and she can pretty much take care of herself. I think it's the fact that she's short and seems quiet and sweet that makes her seem vulnerable. However, as we all know, appearances are usually quite deceiving. The two men wanted a room for the night because it was after 12pm and they did not want to take the chance to drive home. I wasn't sure how far home was. Hilda kept pointing down to the black house phone at the end. I felt that was the end of the help she was extending to them. I tried to help by telling them I would take them down to the phone. They were grateful and came down to the other end. I decided to call for them on the staff phone. I talked with the front desk and gave them the two men's TR numbers. They were gold card members. After checking internal and external, she told me there were no rooms available, not even rooms for which they would pay. She said they had to turn away Diamond and 7-Star players away. Sometimes they have VIP's who reserve a suite of rooms and/or rent the block so they can have the wings to themselves. The front desk person told me that I should suggest they go to the Lounge until they sober up. I told them there were no rooms available and said they could wait in the Lounge area or I could give me taxi information.

Hilda had been there when I was on the phone. She was back at her station when I got off the phone. I went on my computer in the TR info folder to find the taxi phone number. Hilda told me that she had phone numbers. She gave me the taxi phone number and then told me there was a booklet at the end with hotels and their phone numbers. I got all the information and took it down to them. The one who was the most inebriated was on the house phone. I handed him the information and he told me thank you. It was after that Lance told me that one of the things they don't want us to do is interfere when a rep is with a guest because we never know if they are doing a spotlight on a person. He said it might embarrass the rep. I hadn't thought about the spotlight and apologized. Lance said that even when he hears a rep tell a guest the wrong information, he doesn't say anything until they are done and the guest is gone. In the case with Hilda, I felt as though she was done, but you never know what she said to Lance.

People are funny. When I saw Lance later after I'd been counted out, I told him that I thought Hilda was done with the guest and how so many reps had done this to me, that is, interject something or correct me on something, even when I was not done with the rep. He said that he's had to pull them to the side and tell them not to interrupt when he was with a guest. He said it was "hard enough to remember [his] spiel without people interrupting." Later, after talking with my daughter, I realized that although I agreed to some extent with Lance, it seems that the spotlight which was geared more toward us should never take priority over providing the guest with the correct information and the best possible service. It's not about trying to outshine anyone else, at least on my part. I'm all about teamwork and getting things done. However, I have to realize that just because I can do everything doesn't mean I should. I have to remember to allow for others. I have to stop taking over and just let others make their own mistakes. Such is the nature of the office work dynamic and environment.

At lunch break, I ate the spaghetti from two nights before, some cherries, a bread roll, and drank the Vanilla Chai Tea at my locker. The tea tasted like Eggnog. My daughter doesn't like it but I love it. I sat in one of the two-person booths against the right partition in the EDR (Employee Dining Room). I saw Linda with her tray. I thought she was going to join me like she did one other time. I waved to her. She reluctantly waved back. She was looking in front of her and getting a drink from the soft drink machine, and then I saw Ethel. When they both came by I saw Ethel and she said hello.

Alma had been sitting next to me at another small two-person table. Just before she came, Cynthia had come in and sat all the way across the room like she usually does. She will say hello to me but never makes a point to join me. I believe Victoria has put out some bad word on me; either her or someone. Also, maybe they know about my bout with HR for the positions for which I applied. I shared with Alma about my daughter's experience with the Tables Games Training interview. She looked very surprised and told me that she did not have an interview. She said she just put in for her transfer and the manager of the Table Games was her trainer. She said that she had told me before about the department and how they are. She said also that there are some people who won't like you instantly just because of the way you look. She is a Christian woman and usually prays over her food. I like the way she has the blonde weave on her hair. I've heard that some people think blonde hair on a dark-skinned Black woman does not look good, but it's very becoming on her and other dark-skinned women I've seen wear it. Maybe I should go blonde since my hair is turning white-gray anyway. I might consider it. Boy, won't that be something!

Eunice told me about Devin (I believe his name is) who is a Sr. Account Executive Casino Host. She said he's tall and a Black man. She said she's met his wife and daughter. She said I would like him because he's really nice. I told her "they're" nice to you (meaning non-Black women) but not to us. She just smiled and talked about his good qualities. I could tell she knew that I applied for the Sr. Account Executive Casino Host position. I've seen the person to whom she's referring. Hardly any of the Black men in suits will even look at me, let alone say something to me. I notice that Eunice has been cleaning during our shift. I was told that the sunrise shift want to do that because they have nothing to do. So, I just laid out everything to do the embosser cleaning and cleaned some of them. Lance cleaned some of them, as did Charles and Hilda.

I had an incident with a bald Black man in his late 30's or early 40's. He didn't look too thrilled that I was the one who was available to wait on him, something I'd encountered before. I realized that they were thinking like White men now and seeing us the way TV and movies have portrayed us, especially those of who are dark-skinned. He assumed because I was in that position that I was not as educated or articulate as I was. He seemed sort of rude and short with me. I asked him if he wanted someone else to wait on him and he was taken aback. I told him that I was trying to be friendly; he said he didn't want "friendly" he wanted "business." So I said, "Let's start over." I then told him he had $196 in his RC's and that it was worth $98 in cash since he was a Diamond player. He kept asking me why I would be offended. I had already told him I wasn't offended. I was now being business and just business as he had expressed. I repeated again about his comp and cash value. He asked if I was going to answer his question. I told him no and repeated the question as to whether he wanted the $98 in cash. He then said yes. I gave him his slip and he left. He had said he wanted me to be just business and that's what I was; however, he didn't seem to like that either. I didn't bother to tell him about his diamond celebration dinner or the Hidden Jackpot promotion.

When Muriel came in, she asked me how I was doing. I told her, "I can't complain. Well, I can, but I'm not going to." She said, "Yeah, I know what you mean – nobody would listen anyway." She meant it good naturedly. Later, she shook my hand and told me that she heard that congratulations were in order. She said, "You finally made full-time." It seems others were happy for me also. Victoria said that I could get another free shirt for my uniform. I said, "Great," in a wry manner. Muriel said, "Just what you wanted to hear, right?" Victoria commented that they used to get an additional blazer when they wore different uniforms. Tilly had offered to help me go and sign up for my benefits on ESS since we were slow and didn't have anyone in line. Muriel asked me if it was official yet. I asked Muriel whether or not I needed to sign anything. She said that I would just receive something in the mail as confirmation and telling me to sign up for my benefits. At that time, I hadn't received the letter yet.

There are a lot of good laughter times in TR, despite the occasional drama and injustices that go on. A short, Italian male who said he was 53 and a musician, came to my counter and said he had lost his wife. I told him we didn't have any replacement wives, but we do have replacement cards. Sean asked one of the guests if she was feeling lucky. It was an innocent rhetorical question because he was referring to the hidden jackpot promotion where she could swipe her card for free slot play. Victoria kidded him about it being the best pickup line. Later, Victoria encouraged Muriel to go over and ask Sean the same thing. Muriel went over and put her arm around him and said, "Sean, you feeling luck?" His face turned so red and Victoria commented that she'd never seen him turn such a deep color of purple. Hilda was waiting on a gentleman that she said was around his late 30's or early 40's. He was Italian and had salt and pepper hair. After he left, she came over and rolled her tongue in regards to him and said, "Now that's my type." I told her, "Mine too." She relayed this to Victoria. It was interesting how Victoria came back from break later and said she was doing a survey and wanted to know if we ever planned to get married again. She said she was not. I said that it would depend on the person and that God would have to scream at me, "Rachel, this is the one right here and now."

Ethel was there to count us out for the night. I had zero-variance.

Chapter 27

Support Your Neighborhood Sex Addict

July 29 – I called Olga at 12:45pm like she asked me to but she was not there. I didn't leave a message but will continue to call her up until 3pm since I go to work at 4pm. I just might stop in at HR and see if she's there. I finally try to shoo away that black cat that was still hanging around. Since the lady in Unit #1 moved out, the cat has been meowing for us to feed her. I don't want to call the pound because they will put her to sleep, so I just shooed her away. I could hear them cleaning the apartment in Unit #1. I wonder if Luis is planning to move in. Unit #3 appears to be rented by someone in a white pickup truck. Not sure who it is yet. Sara wants to move the bed to the other side of the wall and put the dresser on the other side. She doesn't want to hear them next door. She had also suggested this when we first moved in. She doesn't want them to hear us talking and when I get loud because I'm excited about a subject, she always motions her palm downward so I can take it down a notch. I comply after I spout that I'm in my house.

Chapter 28

For Cherokees Only

I checked the mailbox this morning after I dropped Sara off at work around 8:50am. I wanted to see if they had sent my letter for me to sign offering me a full-time position. There was nothing in the mailbox. I'll check the home mailbox later but they have the PO Box as the mailing for me. I called Olga again at 2pm and left her a message. I also called Helen but did not leave a message for her. I want to ask her if it would be worthwhile to apply for the Cherokee Leader Associate position. I really don't want to waste my time. However, if I don't apply, I'll never know. It's also the timing of everything. I still feel that it will hurt me if I put in for a transfer to apply for the position before I actually sign my papers for the full-time position in TR. I have a feeling it's in their policy somewhere that a change from a part-time to a full-time position cancels any current transfers you have put in. Also, all of a sudden, my full-time position was not finalized, and I won't be made full-time. They are just so shady and deceitful that I don't trust any of them. I trust God, not man. So, I'm asking God to give me wisdom and show me what to do. I have until this coming Thursday on August 1st. It says it closes on Friday, August 2nd but it would be too late. Even if I apply and no one else internal is qualified or applies and there is no 01 who is qualified, they will still just post it external for a tribal member from the outside. I love the Lord with all my heart and know that he is the source of everything I have. I know that if something is for me, I'll get it. I have to look past this present unreal world to what is not seen, that which is truly real. His kingdom is where I belong.

July 30 – Sara checked the mailbox and my letter was there informing me that my employment status changed from part-time to full-time and that I had until August 31st to elect my medical coverage. For a Wednesday, which was one our slow days, the parking lot on the first floor where the buses, vans, and managers park was unusually crowded. I couldn't find a parking space in the Applicant Parking spaces. The only open space was reserved for Maintenance. I reasoned that they may have been conducting New Hire orientation. I parked in front of a lady who looked as if she was waiting for someone. I wasn't comfortable parking there. I went to HR to see if Phoebe was in. There were three people in the waiting room. Helen came out and took the Black man over to the two seats in the next room. I could see them as she crossed her legs across from him and briefly informed him about the position for which he was applying. Sara told me she was. She called her and she said she would be out in a little bit. I waited a few minutes and then told her to let Phoebe know that I had to go move my car and sign up for my benefits.

I went to the computer room. On the way there, I saw Arnette and she was on her 15-minute break. She was in a hurry because she needed to eat her "peanuts" before time was up. There was only one man using the last computer to the far right. He had on one of our front-line uniforms like the one I wear. Victoria had showed me the Monday before the icon on Keyweb that said BORAX on top and PH Leader/SOS beneath. I first tried the SOS icon on the desktop and it did not work. I tried opening the new icon in Keyweb and logged on using my usual information and it did not work.

I went over to IT. Usually I knock; however, I went right in. The geek on duty looked older than the usual techs. I asked him about logging on to the new SOS and he told me my username is the same, but the password would be the last 3 letters of my username plus the last 4 digits of my birthday. He said after I gained access I would then need to change my password, allowing for the fact that my old password is the one I just used (first 3 letters of my username plus the last 4 digits of my social). I went back to the computer room and was able to log on successfully. I noticed that the program had been totally revamped. It was still user-friendly, but contained a lot more information. I noticed that there had been some added features. I asked a woman sitting next to me about the "buy-up." She said her father always told her to get the "buy-up" when it came to insurance because he had a stroke and there were a lot more benefits that he received. She said she always got the dental buy-up because her son needed braces. I elected the dental buy-up because my teeth are sore need of cosmetic repair.

Over 30 years ago when I was with my ex-boyfriend, I had braces. In my ignorance and neglect, of course, I did not feel the need to wear my retainer. Big mistake. The same guy who'd been in the computer room to the far right was still there. However, another young woman with a cheek-length haircut had come in to the use the computer. I noticed she was going through the SOS and was not able to get in. I started telling her how to log in. The guy asked if I'd checked with IT and I told him yes. I noticed that my points said "0" in the system but they were "2" on the attendance books that I'd seen. I also noticed that I had 27 hours of PTO. They tell me I'll earn even more PTO now that I'm full-time.

I left the computer room and stopped back by HR. There was a new person at the desk that I hadn't seen before. I asked about Phoebe and she said Phoebe had gone to lunch and that she wouldn't be back unto 12:30pm. I decided to leave my quest alone for a while. I went up to Brio's to get the Shrimp and Lobster Pasta. It was much better this time. The last time it seemed as though the noodles had been cooked too long. There were three women: one was shorter than the other two, a slight heavier, and was busy writing; one looked pregnant and had short blondish hair; and the other looked young was slim and had long brunette hair. They took my order. While I waited, I was asked how I was doing. I told them that any day I woke up and I was still breathing, it was a good day. The one who had been writing commented how sweet that was and she said she liked my attitude. One of them had the same last name as Felicia. When they asked me my name, I showed them my badge. The one writing had remembered me. I told them I'm one of the people who always recommend Brio's to our guests. She said that I must work with Ivan. I told her yes. She commented on what a great guy he was and that he just won the Leadership Award. I said yes, he was a good guy. Of course, I thought so at the time. She asked me if I knew Felicia and I told her that Felicia was my supervisor. She said that she loved Felicia and had tried to set her up with her father. I asked her if her father was younger because Felicia likes younger men. She asked me if I was planning to stay in TR. I said I liked it there but that "you never know." She said that it was great money. I told her that I'd made $54,000 a year. Her eyes cast down and asked me what I had done. I explained that I'd taught high school and adult education, had worked in Personnel for 6 years, and had my own Adult Education/GED program.

It always amazes me that most White people pre-judge me because of what I look like. Most of it is preconditioning from TV and movies, etc. It was a safe assumption on her part, so I couldn't resent her for it. The average pay in the casino industry is minimum wage, and my position pays a little more than $3 more than that minimum wage. What a travesty! They pull in billions of dollars and one of the main types of positions that bring in the immediate funds (table games dealers) only gets $5.25 plus tips. It is the tips that bring their pay up to maybe $20 to $25 an hour. I had never been one given to tipping. My reasoning was that employers should pay their workers what they deserve and not rely on the customers/guests to pay their workers' salaries. A tip is a gratuity, that is, something I give of my own freewill, if and when I want to. This is why I resent restaurants that not only add the tip in the bill, but they increased it from 10% to 15%. The 10% came from the Bible, for example, tithing. The secular world uses the same principle in a commercial way and then tacks on another 5%. Apparently, it got so good, that the IRS decided to get in on the action, even though the practice was unconstitutional. It's called Income Tax. They decided they should receive 15% tip also. When you get paid, they get paid. Today, their tip has grown to 30% and may just get higher. One of the problems I have with the government taking a tip, is I haven't figured out just what service they provide that I've actually asked for. I guess I should thank them for harassing me when I'm driving down the street and didn't pay them for the privilege of driving my car down "their" streets or get mandatory insurance. I guess I should thank them for providing me with libraries, parks, and other government buildings that are not available to be 24/7 and that I cannot use without their permission. I guess I should thank them for providing laws and regulations where people like George Zimmerman (a White man) can go free after shooting an unarmed young Black man and giving 20 years to a Black woman who shot a gun in the air to scare away her abusive ex-husband who was trying to attack her. Travon Martin is dead. George Zimmerman walks away free, and the Black woman is serving her sentence while her abusive husband has custody of her children. I guess I should especially thank the Obama Administration for putting a health care plan into place that none of the people voted for, whereby I have to have medical insurance or else I'll incur a federal fine after January 1 of next year. It is just another ironic testament to the fact that we no longer have any individual freedoms in America, "land of the free." This is my body, but the government says I have to have medical insurance. This is just a precursor to the future when they will mandate that I have to take their drugs and get their flu shots. What terrible times are coming!

I didn't dawn on me to ask my daughter if she wanted anything from Brio's because she doesn't like their food for the price. However, I apologized to her later because I didn't even ask her if she wanted anything else. She said it was okay because she was sleepy and went back to bed, but I felt awful. She always asks me if I want anything.

I stopped by TR Motor Coach area to get Jack to sign my transfer slip because I wanted to apply for the Cherokee Leader Associate position. Alexis was down there with him and she remarked how good Brio's food is. Jack sighed and signed the transfer sheet and told me that I'd have to get Ivan to sign it. He called Ivan who was not there. Jack said that Ivan came in at 11am. I told him that he (Jack) had me coming in at 12 noon the next day, so I would talk with Ivan then. I realized that Jack's job is not easy when he has a schedule, just changed my status, and Arnette's, and then we put in for transfers. Arnette just might get her position because she said the other day Ivan was actually working to help her get an interview with the hiring manager for the part-time position in the Service Center on the 3rd floor. However, I have a feeling my situation may not be the same.

Chapter 29

I Don't Know, What Do You Want To Do?

I play my Bejeweled 2 game in the evenings. There is an ever-increasing number of Reality shows on TV, the movies are not good, the sitcoms are stupid, and I just don't find pleasure in much of what they put on for us to watch. Sometimes I literally hate it. However, just when I think I'm going to upchuck, I see that *Touched by An Angel* with Roma Downey, Della Reese, John Dye, and Valerie Bertinelli is on. I love the episodes. There was one with Angela Lansbury and another with Luther Vandross. The episodes always touch my heart because they talk about God's love and forgiveness, and the hero and/or heroine always have an epiphany at the end. It's a shame the show is only in syndication.

One thing I realize is that many of the wonderful writers have passed on. I go back and watch on the Internet YouTube videos where Halle Berry, Viola Davis, and Susan Lucci win their Oscars, SAG, and/or NAACP Award. It's the humanity and touching emotion that gets to me. I watch Whitney Houston and Michael Jackson. It's not all of their videos, just the ones where "moments in time" were important because of what was going in their lives. There are a handful of people that I wish I could just go back and talk with before they died. I realize that I am really nobody in this world and in the big scheme of things. Sometimes I wish I could make good positive impacts on the lives of others. Maybe that's why I write. I'm still that little girl who used to pray every night before going to bed that God would make everyone happy. No one except my daughter knows that one of my bucket list items is to do stand-up comedy, to sing, and to act. I wanted to be an entertainer when I was younger, but God had other plans. Somehow I feel that he wanted me to first seek his kingdom and his righteousness, and then all else would be added unto me, as his Word says. If he opens the door, I'll step into it and be the best that I can be, for him and for his glory.

Arnette called while I was trying to watch *Touched by An Angel* with Luther Vandross. I was trying to balance listening to what she was saying and listen to Luther and Della Reese sing "I Believe." Sara found it on YouTube after this. Arnette said she was going to go to the Employee Appreciation picnic after all and would see me there. She asked what time I would be there and I told her I'd find out tomorrow because I didn't even know what the picnic times were.

My daughter and I had a disagreement over the poker tournaments that she wants to attend in Jacksonville. Whenever I think about playing poker or slots or anything to do with gambling anymore, I have this sick feeling inside my stomach. It's odd because a friend tried to tell me this a long time ago. He said that he'd gotten this way after placing his last bet. He talked about how the gambling had almost destroyed him. Some of us have to learn for ourselves. I believe my daughter will too. I don't want her to make the 7-hour trip by herself, so if I end up going with her but spend most of my time in the hotel room with my computer, my Bible, my God, and the host of angels around me. It's like an alcoholic staying near a place where they're offering all the booze you can buy.

I understand people with addictions, especially when you have two people who feed off each other's addictions. Gambling has destroyed so many good things in my life, whether it was me or it was my daughter – either way, God made me realize that my blessings were being stopped because of it. I'm going to make a stand against it as long as I can; however, if she insists on going, I'll have to make a decision. I told her I wished she would focus on the gifts God has given her and I know that one of them is writing. She just wants to play poker and win tournaments so she can play poker tournaments and poker cash games. I believe she will be very philanthropic and help a lot of people, but I'm so afraid she'll expend all her money in desperation to win and then not win. I just don't want her to experience more and more heartache in an arena of which I don't believe God approves. Of course, I don't know everything. Only God knows for sure. I know we have to allow our children to make their own mistakes, no matter how much we love them and want to protect them. God does us the same way. I feel so bad because I know my daughter would go with me if I had to make a long trip by myself. In fact, she did. It seems she's made some sacrifices for me. She trusted my judgment, so I'll have to trust hers. I think it's my own insecurities when it comes to the gambling, I don't trust. God help me to be a good steward with what you have provided.

Chapter 30

Some People Never Learn

August 1 – I rode in with Sara who went in at 11am. I took all of my papers, my transfer application for the Cherokee Leader Associate position, my resume, and my transcripts from ASU and Univ. of Phoenix again – all were attached. I went into Ivan's office to get it signed. I didn't expect him to go out of his way for me as he had done Arnette. He asked about the job description and I told him it was listed as an internship and that you would be working with a lot of different departments and doing different things. I said that I had done a lot of different things. He agreed as he looked at my resume.

I remember that it was the first time he'd really seen it. I said that I feel that I might be able to make some contributions because program improvement is in my background since I was a Nationally Certified Manager of Program Improvement through the Ariz. Dept. of Education when I served as Executive Director for the Waiting To Excel Education Center Adult Education/GED Program for three years. He said surprised, "You've done recruiting?" I told him "Yes – also at Motorola." I told him that I'd done recruiting and conducted New Hire Orientation while at Motorola, in addition to working in Personnel for 6 years. I told him that they usually want you to keep your resume to two pages so I didn't include everything. He said that the position description was probably on Keyweb and he went on there to look it up. He sat there and read through it carefully. He said that he knew someone else who was interested in the position. I think this whole process was truly unprofessional.

Sometimes managers have selfish goals; therefore, they can either positively or negatively affect the outcome of whether or not you get a particular position. Though I know I'm qualified and can do the job, I still have to allow God to work it out for me. I told Ivan that you have to have a Bachelor's Degree and he said, "Oh, you do have to have a Bachelor's." I didn't tell him that I knew that one of the Cage Cashiers in Randy's department had wanted the position and told Randy she was going to apply for it. Sara said that Randy had told her that "I'm the one to know." Apparently he was going to help her. Sara said that the cashier later said she had decided not to apply. I told Ivan that I had passed Superlap. He wanted to know what "ESO" meant. I told him I didn't know. He called someone on the phone who sounded like Edward and asked Ivan asked him the same question. The person said he didn't know. Ivan said, "Call me back." Why would they put an acronym on a job description without putting in parentheses what it meant? If they can't find someone else internal for the position, they will try to eliminate me from the running by saying I haven't taken ESO. The ESO was included with the Superlap. I found out later that ESO was the class they took: Exploring Supervisory Opportunities.

They know that I'm qualified and more so for the position. If they can at all prevent me from interviewing for it, they will. However, should I get an interview they will find a way to reject me, if they can. This is all in my Father's hands. The devil is at work but he's not more powerful than The Most High Father Yahweh. I told Ivan that I didn't want him to think that I didn't like working there, because I do like working there, and I like the people with whom I work. However, I told him the position would allow me to do a great deal of other things. I told him that the job I'm in now is different; not a negative difference – just different. I told him it was the first job I'd had where I punched a time clock, worked weekends and wore a uniform. I asked him what he thought about the position and me in it. He never really answered; however, I told him that I wasn't sure if they wanted a younger person who was up and coming. I told him that when they ask the question "How do you see yourself in 10 years?" that I know what they're looking for because I've interviewed people before; however, I have to answer honestly and say that because I'm pushing 60, I see myself retired in 10 years. He commented that he was also looking forward to when he could retire. He finally signed the papers and told me he was going down to HR to drop off another application so he could turn it in. He then asked, "Unless you want to turn it in yourself?" I told him that it was fine if he turned it in and that it was due at 4pm that day. I saw him put it in a manila envelope. He asked me if there was anything else, and I told him no and he told me to have a good day. I said good bye.

Today Jack scheduled me to come in at 12 noon again. Both he and Edward and Carol were there during Buzz. I could tell that Ivan had shared with Edward about my application, my background, and my experience. I realize now that they all know that I'm a force to be reckoned with and that possibly there might be another opening in the department. I couldn't tell which was bothering them more. Edward went over quickly what was on the board. I was sitting down and asked if they'd told everyone about the new login for the SOS system. Edward said that yes it was on Keyweb. He said the login was the first 2 digits of your username plus the . . ." He interrupted himself and I corrected him. Jack chimed in and repeated what I just said. Sometimes I really feel like a misfit. I know that my abilities and qualifications surpass the positions I end up in; however, I need to have the basic necessities in life and must sustain my existence. When will my opportunity come? Edward sent Carol upstairs and told me to go to the Rotunda.

We had very little staff that day. When I went down to the Rotunda, I saw that there were no cords for the players' cards and the Gold level cards had no holes in them. I didn't understand what was going on at the time. I just told the guests that there were no bungee cords and no holes for the Gold cards. I apologized in advance to them. Alice was there.

She is such a sweet person. I remember sharing with her about Pastor Boyd, how he was dying of cancer and yet, every time I asked him how he was doing he would just say, "Fine." Until one day when I asked him why he always said that when I knew he was in pain most of the time. He said, "Because if it's not fine, it will be." I told Alice that I wanted to perfect that same attitude one day and not complain. She said that she did also. It was a real slow day. I realize that when I'm out on Tuesday and Wednesday I miss out on a lot. Sometimes the supervisors forget who heard what in Buzz and don't always repeat the information. They should probably write down everything they share. I know they try, but somehow the ball gets dropped at times. It happens to everyone. I took a 15-minute break. When it came time for my usual 30-minute break, I called on the radio for a TR supervisor. I got Ethel. I asked if it was okay to take a 30. She said okay. However, when I got down to the restroom area, I realized that I was only going to be there until 6:30, that is, a 6-hour day. I took 13 minutes and then went into the Buzz area, hoping that Ethel would be there. She was there and so was Louise. I noticed that Louise still does not look me directly in the eye. Ethel did not really turn around. She heard my voice so she knew it was me, but I still thought this was rude. I said, "Ethel, I made a mistake. I'm only here for 6 hours so I just took a 15, not a 30." She said, "Okay, thank you ma'am." It was pretty deserted in the casino that day until later.

Chapter 31

Brother, Can You Spare a Coupon?

August 2 – We're still offering the choice of 4 different gifts for the Property Acquisition promotion. It will continue through the end of August. I keep wondering what they're working on for the month of September. Jack made my schedule pretty much the same for this week. However, I notice that Beverly and Zelda get to work at least 2 hours earlier than I do. I know this is not by accident. It seems the Indian Preference Act extends to a lot more than what it was intended. It did not intend for them to have preference in schedules, but they seem to enjoy this benefit also. God will work it all out for my good.

Ivan was down there during Buzz. Ethel went over a few things then she said that one of the guests brought in a coupon from Atlantic City that had expired but the rep did not notice that the coupon was from Atlantic City. Before she could finish I told her that it was me because I remembered someone bringing in a coupon from Atlantic City. The guest said that it didn't work in the machine. I believe it was Mary who was sitting next to me who had noticed that the coupon said Atlantic City. She called it to our attention. The guest said that they had called and someone told them they could use the coupon. I told the guest that our other properties will allow Cherokee coupons to be used at their facility, but that we don't reciprocate.

Ivan talked to everyone about the fact that Cherokee hit $50 million in one month and that no other casino except the big one in Las Vegas had ever done this. He talked about the Jackpot Bonus and that we were on target to reach it by the end of the year. We were at 63% and needed to be at 68% for our OS (Overall Score). He said that FH (Friendly/Helpful) was good but that our WT (Wait Time) was down. He said our K (Knowledge) was pretty good, but our OS needed to come up. He encouraged us to do everything we're supposed to with a guest, but that if we can't provide a guest with what they want at the time, we should offer them something else. He said we should leave them with a pleasant experience, that is, hopefully to have a smile on their faces when they leave. I had told him in the meeting with him and Felicia a month ago that I had been doing this. He said that if we reached the mark, we would all receive 10,000 RC's. He said he's been told that this was enough to purchase an iPad. I said, "Oh really?" I have been wanting (not needing) an iPad for a while now. I said, "So what I hear you telling us is that we're getting raises?" with a smile on my face. Little did I know how ironic this would be later when everyone except me would receive a raise in pay. He said, "If you're still here, yes next year you would get an annual raise." He didn't know that I was not referring to the Jackpot Bonus but the fact that the casino had made $50 million in one month. The raise I was talking about was meant for everyone who works at the casino, not just our department. However, little did I know that he had already planned for me not to be there next year.

Ivan was going to have to work in Valet because he was short-staffed. So, he asked if any of us wanted to go park cars. Sean said he would. He said he would help out wherever he was needed. I commented how Ivan leads by example and that if he could park cars. so could we. Ethel agreed.

I was at the Rotunda again from 6pm to 2:30am. The casino was packed again. The Black Crowe's concert did bring a few new people in. Most of the guests I waited on were not that impressed with the concert. I noticed that many of the guests were drunk and they ended up at my counter. One guest said he worked in the Entertainment/Restaurant business but he said he couldn't tell me where he worked. It didn't dawn on me until just now as I'm writing this that it must have been Paula Deen's. Her brand had now been replaced with Selu Gardens Café. Ivan had reminded us to tell people it was a café so they would know that it was casual dress. He even provided us with menus at our stations. I glanced over the menu and didn't see anything that stood out. Of course, I'm prejudiced toward anything with lobster and I didn't see that on the menu. The highest amount I gave away in Hidden Jackpot free slot play was $75. People weren't winning the big amounts anymore. A guest mentioned that the wins were probably based on your play, but it hadn't dawned on me. It's supposed to be random, but I keep wondering if there is some way for them to rig it so that it's triggered to give players with higher C.A.P. scores a bigger amount of slot play. However, I decided this was not the case because Diamonds and 7-Star guests were getting low slot play and God and Platinum guests were getting high slot play.

It appeared to be completely random. Some of the guests were just receiving bonus entries into the August 25th drawing. I did overhear one of the other reps (Carol, I believe) talk about the August 25th drawing and that there would be an increasing cash amount given away every hour. I always remembered to tell the guests about the October 2nd drawing where a trip to Vegas would be given away and the $1 million dollars given to one person. I still, for the life of me, cannot figure out why they insist on giving out such a large amount to only one person – that is, until I made a comment that I loved giving away money. This was right after I had just redeemed a $100 free slot play coupon. One of the other reps said, "Especially when it's not yours." I told the rep that I've even given away my own money. I wish I had tons of money just to given away to people. However, I know that money is not the answer to all of their problems. It helps, but people need the Lord, Jehovah Jireh, our provider. He will supply all of our needs and even give us some of our wants.

Chapter 32

7-Star and Diamond for a Day

Linda was leaving as I was coming back from my break. I noticed that the 7-Star chair was the only one that was open except for the ones at the end. I noticed that there were quite a few guests in line. After the line had greatly reduced, I was waiting on a guest and his companion. The guest was from California. His license did not scan so I input some of his information. I noticed that his license had expired and I apologized to him that I would be unable to create an account and issue him a card because his license had expired. I never got the chance to tell him that I would create an account for his companion who had an Alien Registration Card and that I could give her two cards. However, I would have to assess whether or not he looked over 30 and make a decision based on this. He told me his license had been updated online which is one way California will allow you to update your driver's license. He said it was in an email. I told him that he had to bring that in with him also. He said that what I was telling him is that he needed a computer and a printer. He asked if we had that. Before I could answer, I noticed that Ethel must have been standing behind me. She took the card out of my left hand and told him, "Here's the deal. We can't issue a license with an expired license." She told him that the card she had in her hand was not updated and that's what we had to go by. I asked him if he wanted me to create an account for his friend. He said, "If I'm not going to gamble here, she's not going to gamble here." He was leaving but Ethel did tell him that he didn't need a card to gamble. However, he was no longer listening.

I could feel vibes that Ethel didn't agree with me sitting in the 7-Star chair. I think Tilly is the one who had seniority of the reps there at the time and she was in the 4th seat. However, no one said anything to me. When I came back from my last break, Barbara was in the 7-Star seat and I went down to the other end. Felicia, who had been in the Diamond chair, called me to sit there. I see the difference when you're humble and not assert yourself. It's like the Bible says, that you should not "come up hither" unless you are called. It says it was better to wait until this happens because you may be embarrassed when someone calls you down from a high position. I was reminded of this when three months ago when Felicia said she was going to take me out of the 7-Star chair. I was sitting there only because someone else told me to sit there. This was when Felicia was still a D/R Supervisor.

I think working at the casino has cured me from ever wanting to play slots and table games again. I feel a sick feeling in my gut when I think of even placing one bet and I don't even want to buy scratchers or other lottery tickets. I'm content with my minimal stock investing. This is about as much gambling as I want to do. I know that God is all-knowing. He puts us where he wants us to learn something and at times, he even has multiple purposes. It was my friend who works at Gila River Indian Casino, who told me, "You haven't written the book you're supposed to yet. Who knows what your experiences may bring. Your book may help the big wigs see everything from a different perspective – because you're on the front line and see and know what's going on. You are their eyes and ears." It's interesting he would say this because I'm also God's eyes and ears, along with his hands. I'm his representative. I'm here for his purpose. My gift is writing and I use it for his purpose, not my own.

Chapter 33

The Dark Side

August 3 – Today's events reminded me of the foreboding I had about a week ago. I had such a good time in the Lord a few days ago where I ended up praising God in the spirit and in song that was in tongues of a Native American dialect. I don't know their language, so I'm unaware of what it was. I remember giving my life completely and totally over to God to be used by him. I am his tool. It's not easy being God's tool. You are hated and hunted by the devil and his forces. It truly is a spiritual battle. Sometimes things looked at in retrospect can give you understanding of specific events and how and why people acted the way they did. I didn't bring much to eat that day, just mixed nuts and some cherries and a piece of Swiss cheese. I usually bring yogurt (Activia) for my first break, but did not bring the yogurt that day. I put the Red Beans in a pot of water (after washing them) on the stove so they could swell. I left a note for Sara so she could cook them. I learned some time ago that if you do this first with beans, it takes less cooking time to get them done. I didn't feel as well as I liked but I wrote in this journal the events that happened the day before, as usual. I also listened to gospel music. I was concerned about running out of gas after taking Sara to work; however, I decided to chance it and get gas sometime before I go to work. When I dropped Sara off at work, I noticed Poindexter sitting outside waiting for the Motor Coaches. Even though I had my glasses on, I believe he noticed me. I saw him out of the corner of my eye, but did not attempt to let him know I saw him.

I had been noticing Zelda's manner had been stand-offish but today it seemed even more so. It was as if she was avoiding any conversation with me. I couldn't understand because it was so different from the way it had been before. I remember the other day, however, when we were both down at the

Rotunda, she commented that she couldn't understand why they won't allow us to be in the EDR when we're off duty and/or more than an hour before or after our shift starts. I told her that something must have happened and she agreed. It seems that when one incident, however small, occurs there, the "powers that be" seem to react rather than pro-act before something negative occurs.

Ethel did the Buzz and she said it was busy out there. Ivan was down there and he said, "How you doing Rachel?" I told him I was doing great and asked how he was. I was feeling good that day. Ethel talked about Jack's upcoming BBQ for the TR department. It was written on the slate they use for the Buzz meetings. It was coming up on August 10th on the 3rd Floor. Until the events that ensued after this, I was looking forward to it. I did not get to take my first 15-minute break until almost a quarter of 7. I was called into a meeting with Felicia and I was surprised that Ethel was in there. I realized that something must be up. Felicia gave me 2 write-ups. The first one was regarding the Black guy who had come in previously and did not seem like he wanted me to wait on him. Apparently he had left my counter after I'd given him his receipt for the $98 in cash to redeem from the cashier's cage.

He went over to the cage cashier and asked to speak to a supervisor. He must have thought the departments were all the same. The email to Ivan (dated July 28) said that I had been rude and unprofessional and that I had refused to wait on him. Of course, it was all untrue; however, I explained to Felicia what happened. Ethel asked what he wanted. I told her he wanted to cash out his reward credits. The email said the guy said he was more tired and weary. I may have mistaken his fatigue and weariness for not wanting me to wait on him, so I told Felicia that I would take responsibility for that one. The other one she said was more serious in nature. While the first one had been a verbal coaching, the second one came with a documented coaching. The word "verbal" had been scratched out and the word "documented" was put on it. I believe Ethel had her put this, or maybe Ivan did. The email was from Bertha to Ivan and was dated July 30. Bertha said that I had been increasingly aggressive and rude to her. There was even capitalized letters to represent that I had shouted at her. She made comments in her email and reference to a conversation that she and I never had. It had been with Olga in HR. This is when I knew they had talked about me and with each other. It was as if they knew if Bertha, who is a manager, wrote the email, it would carry a lot more weight. I told Felicia that it was all a lot of "bunk." I couldn't believe what I was hearing and reading. I started to object, and Felicia told me she was just doing her job. I told her that it was unfair to get a write-up when no one challenged that she was not telling the truth. Felicia said that Bertha had been at Harrah's for a long time and they'd never known her not to write something like that unless something happened.

Did it ever occur to any of them that maybe they don't want me to promote and/or to get any positions? Whenever you are an intelligent Black woman, educated, self-assertive and capable, the only thing they can come up with to hold you back is say it's your "attitude" or your "tone." Like my daughter says, it's always something abstract and not something concrete. It's always so subjective. So much for being free. I remember saying, "Satan, I rebuke you in the name of Jesus!" I said, "Why are they doing this?" and "Well, I know why." I just shook my head and sighed. I said I needed to have a meeting with her (Bertha) and then Felicia and Ethel gave me two numbers of people to talk to in Employee Relations (Dixie and Alexandria). I had called over a month or so ago to talk to Alexandria returned my call, but I never called them back. Felicia and Ethel said that I could make comments on the write-ups. I told them I would have to write something up. So, I wrote on there "Will make comments later" on both of them. Felicia said I could go on my 15-

minute break. She made a comment that if I wasn't coming back to let her know. I said, "Felicia, I wouldn't do that." As I was leaving, I told them, "I guess the bottom line is you shouldn't ask questions."

It occurred to me that someone or several people wanted to see me fired – or at least silenced. I spoke briefly with one of the Black women who were dealers. One was older and used to be a supervisor and the other one was Alma. I couldn't talk much with Alma because a table games supervisor came into the EDR quiet room where we were. Alma said that she does research on the positions before she applies and knows who to talk to. She said she told me before that there is so much politics that go on and that she hates it. The other lady said that they always do "us" (meaning Black people) that way. I told her that it didn't seem like they do Black men that way because I see them in VIP Host and Sr. Acct. Exec. Casino Host positions. She said they do them that way also. I think she may have been thinking about Travon Martin. There are such tensions in Florida and I think I now know why the policies and procedures have been changing there. People are running scared for some reason. However, I believe they're running from their own demons.

Although I think it was unfair of them to give me the write-ups a few hours into my shift, I was able to pray my way through. Most of them don't serve the God I do, so they don't know how to handle these things. I was still calm and professional in my manner. I was the same friendly person I usually am to my co-workers and to the guests. I mentioned to Jeffrey briefly about what was being done to me. He said, "Now you want to hear my story?" I wanted to talk with him except people were coming in line. I now understand a great deal. Everyone there, in some form or fashion, has been treated so badly. It's really not so much race as with regard to being treated as a low-caste employee. I need to ask about the circus training. I've been told that I'm scheduled for August

24th. However, the information in the Daily News says we need to sign up for it. I will check with Felicia on tomorrow.

My daughter told me that they denied her PTO. She said that I would be happy about it but she was not. She said that everyone there has been approved for their PTO. They told her that it was a holiday (Labor Day) weekend and was a mandatory work weekend. However, she said she keeps trying to cancel the previous PTO and that they may make her take it. Apparently, it won't delete out of the system. She's right that I didn't want her to go to Jacksonville by herself, but I was not happy the way they are treating her. They know that I am manager material and want to make sure that I don't even make it to a supervisory level. I dared to ask questions because they never do any follow-up and there is such lack of communication in addition to misinformation. Brad agreed with me when I commented to him about the lack of communication and miscommunication in that whole place.

I realize that they are afraid of me, that is, afraid I'm going to try to change their status quo. I know that I'm dealing with spiritual wickedness in high places. Father in Heaven, please show up and show out. Lead and guide me as to what to do. You tell us to be wise as a serpent and harmless as a dove. However, you say in your word that we have to take what belongs to us. I have decided to do several things: 1) do most of my communication in writing; 2) request a copy of my Personnel file (all of it), that which is in my department and that which HR holds. I will do this in an official manner with a copy to the Tribal Gaming Commission and Caesar's Entertainment, that is, a copy to Mendleson. They want me to be busy with fighting to get the write-ups out of my file so that in the meantime, I can't successfully apply for and get any of the positions. I must have been lied to by Helen during New Employee Orientation. There is so much corruption at that place that I don't know where to begin. The battle is not mine; it's the Lord's. He will go before me.

August 4 – Even though I was shocked and disappointed yesterday evening after the write-ups, to say the least, today I felt more of the impact. I believe God allowed me to be more controlled so that I didn't break down in front of the guests and that I could successfully do my job. I realized that they were trying to get me to "shut up" and not ask questions. I talked to my friend who works at Gila River Indian Casino. I told him about what was going on. I told him that yes, he was right, God did want me to write a book. However, I know that there is something more I'm supposed to do. I shared with him the information I'd found regarding the Indian Preference Act of 1934, how it was changed in 1974 and signed by our "Black representative" in the Supreme Court, Clarence Thomas. It was changed to extend the range of their preferences in employment; however, they have also used the preferences to include everything else, including shift schedules and going from part-time to full-time. I told him, as I told my daughter: I'm just so tired now. I've been working full-time since I was 18 years old (almost 40 years) and I've dealt with this stuff so much. I wrote about the majority of them in a book I published called "Will Work for Food, Family & Freedom." When I wrote it, I thought I'd never be working for anyone else again. I was wrong.

My friend asked me if I really wanted to work there (at the casino). I told him that at this point, I really had no choice. I told him how I had applied for countless jobs in Georgia: through the public school system, through the County, through the State, through several private sectors, and through several non-profit organizations. I applied through the County here in North Carolina. In fact, I applied for close to 10 positions for which I was qualified, some for which I was over-qualified. I applied for teaching positions. In the end, I couldn't believe that the only opportunities would be a tutoring position where I had to drive a long distance several times a week, either to a student's home or the library.

My daughter would only get a part-time job in Georgia working at Taco Bell where she had to drive a long distance, getting paid minimum wage ($7.25 an hour). They were "training" her to be a shift manager where she would, after 6 months they said, get an extra $1 an hour. In the meantime, she came home with her back and feet hurting because they had her washing and cleaning everything and sweeping and mopping floors. My daughter tells me about (and I can see) the number of young people who work there and have been there for several years. There are those who were hired when they were 18 years old and now been there for 16 years – and a lot of them are not Natives. They are also not Black people; they are of European descent. So, here I am, I told my friend, I finally have a job with benefits, and I had to fight for that. They know that I need the benefits and the job because of my age. Because of my age – this is the part of the bottom line as to why I was getting rejection after rejection and no responses to the countless jobs for which I applied. It took me a while to realize that not many companies want to hire older workers like me who will not doubt, if they live long enough, be retired in 10 years. I know that the only reason they hired me at Harrah's was because: 1) they really needed people; 2) I was over-qualified; 3) I said I would work any shift (Ethel who conducted my interview, really stressed this); 4) I answered the last question to the point that she said, "Wow, that's the best I've ever seen."

A friend told me that Caesar's Entertainment doesn't care and that they know that I can "be replaced." I shared with him how they re-branded Paula Deen's Kitchen because of the controversy behind her alleged use of the N-word. Apparently the complaint had been brought against Paul Deen personally. According to the rumor, she admitted that she used the word in the past and when asked if she thought the word could be offensive to some people, she apparently did not answer along lines thought to be politically correct. It's amazing to me how many White people who came into TR and discussed it briefly said she should have lied. I told them I didn't condone lying, but I thought she could have been a bit more diplomatic in her answer. So, I told my friend, if Harrah's and Caesar's Entertainment (and apparently the Tribe) can take action that way and instruct us to say, "Harrah's does not discriminate," then surely they will have to own up to what they say. The truth is they allow the Tribe to discriminate – and big time. Even with everything else, the 01 Preference does not bother me half as much as the fact that they will only allow a few Blacks in but not in high level positions whereby they are promoted from within. More importantly, the Blacks they allow in high level positions have never been a Black woman. My friend ended up telling me that he will definitely pray for me in this situation.

Chapter 34

Pray While They Prey

Even though I had prayed and read my word, I needed human comfort. I had already dropped my daughter off at work; however I had tried to reach Arnette that morning, but I usually get a message that "The Magic Jack customer you have called is not available." I think I may have to show Arnette how to set up her voice mail. I called Louise and left her a message. I remembered that it was Sunday and that she would be either at church or somewhere enjoying her weekend. I thought several times about calling my mother, my father, or even Marilyn, but decided against it. I felt that Marilyn had heard enough of my trials and my parents would just feel that it's the same thing over again.

I prayed some more and talked with God. I just couldn't understand why I have to be the one to take the stand. I remember telling my daughter that I had once again, given my total and complete life over to God for his purposes. I know I was put in this specific place and time for his purposes. He allowed other doors to close but left this one open. Now that he's placed me there, I'll be there for his purpose and for his time. The enemy keeps us at odds with each other all of the time. The bottom line is that "injustice anywhere is a threat to justice everywhere." The devil appeals to the selfish greed of non-regenerated and unrepentant humans who have not had their sins washed in the blood of Christ. Sin has no color, race, or creed barrier. It encompasses all. This is how the devil keeps us all fighting against each other. This spiritual wickedness in high places is so clever and crafty, so calculating and so scheming, yet ever so undercover that only those who are wise in God and have rejected the foolishness of the world, even understand what is going on.

I went in about 25 minutes early, and I saw Ethel down the hall. She said hello, but I just waved. I also saw Arnette and she was in a hurry because she was on her way back from break. I know that she's under a lot of pressure also. I told her briefly about the 2 write-ups. She told me to email her and that we would pray.

In the Buzz were Nicholas, Ethel, Eunice, and eventually Linda came in. Ethel asked if there was anything new and exciting going on like she usually did. No one really said much. Eunice asked me how I was doing and I just waved and didn't really answer. I listened half-heartedly to what they were all saying. Nicholas was saying that there would be no team tournament events at the Employee Appreciation picnic. At first, Ethel thought he meant that the picnic was cancelled. She commented how one year they had everyone sign up and made all of the arrangements and procured all of the food and decorations, and only 12 people showed up. I was now starting to understand why about 75-80 percent of the people there were unhappy, cynical, and walked around with their heads down. Most of them just smiled when they saw a friendly face, a familiar face, or a supervisor/manager (especially Mendleson).

I now understand why they wear "fake smiles" when with guests. Alma told me later that day that you have to have thick skin to work there. She told me later in EDR that as a table games dealer you have to put up with abuse. I said, "Verbal?" and she looked at me and told me it was all kinds of abuse. She said she knew dealers who have been spit on and they have to take it. I told her that Zelda used to be a dealer and she said that when people were playing $400 a hand and spending their money, you have to put up with whatever they dish out. I guess this is one of the reasons she transferred to TR. Alma and my daughter both told me that working there could cause you to lose your morals because it is so corrupt and so much goes on behind the scenes that would boggle the mind.

I noticed in Buzz that I had moved down in number of transactions on the July 1 through July 31 sheet. It now just says Efficiency sheet. My daughter told me they've scheduled her to get her 4-10's back and she will still work day hours. It's very hard on me but I'm glad she has the hours and shift she wants.

I was so down and quiet in the Rotunda. Zelda was saying something to me, but I just made a motion with my finger going across my lips as if to signify that my lips were sealed. Linda asked if I wanted to sit in the 7-Star chair. I told her that Barbara might want to sit there when she gets back. She asked me if I felt all right and I just shrugged my shoulders. Later, I went in and shared with what happened in my getting the two write-ups. I couldn't hold it and I cried some. I told her that it "just hurts" what they did. She hugged me. She was very encouraging. She told me how she had been done the same way a while back in another department. She said there were 4 supervisors in there and she felt as though she had been flanked on every side. She said she broke down and cried. I told her I could take it if they tell me that I didn't get the job because they wanted someone else, or they felt I was not the best fit for their department, or something. However, when they are so devious and lie and defame my character just for their own selfish ends so that I can't ever move upward or forward, it's very hard to take, especially since I've gone through this time and time again.

Enough is enough! There is going to come a time when you just have to stop going around the road blocks and start busting them down because it's not always about yourself; it's about others who come after you and will encounter those same roadblocks. What happens when there are no more ways around the roadblocks? However, I do believe that in those days and times God will miraculously lift you up and out of the situation.

Linda said that she heard that Employee Relations is no help at all. I told her that Felicia and Ethel were both in the meeting and she said that they both worked hand in hand. I can feel that Linda knows that Felicia gossips and doesn't really trust her or Ethel to the fullest. I understand by some of the things Linda says and does not say.

After the talk with Linda I felt a bit better. She told me things were going to get better and to just hang in there. She told me how she had to just "suck it up" and keep moving. However, she, along with countless others, has learned to just be quiet and keep your head low. I also believe that God will not always allow me to do this. For God's plans and ways are not always the same as ours.

I saw Luis in the Quiet Room of the EDR and told him briefly about what was going on. I noticed he has been wearing his uniform quite a bit instead of his suit. He was talking very low so I only got the gist of what he was saying. He told me that since the road was blocked that I should take around route. He told me to contact Pablo in the Credit Dept. I asked if he was a Black guy. He said yes and that Pablo was also working on something for him, but he might find something for me. I believe God arranges things and sets appointments. I believe it was no accident that when I was going through the casino door to the back house, Pablo was coming in at the same time. I told him that Luis had asked me to talk to him. He gave me his card and told me to email him.

I get such bad vibes from Tilly at work. She smiles but I'm reminded of the scripture that says flattering words are on their lips but there is war in their hearts. She asked me about one of the Combines that I printed out. I printed out two sheets for the two accounts. They don't let me do Combines anymore so I couldn't do it so it wouldn't confuse anybody. I notice that she had taken the sheets to Muriel.

When Muriel asked me about it, I told her that the lady wanted the account on the second page as her account and it had the correct information. Muriel said that it really doesn't work that way. Linda had been in there to hear the conversation. It was 12:15 am and I was really tired. I told Muriel that my brain wasn't really working at that time to remember. She seemed in a negative and evil mood. Linda told me later that they are now giving write-ups for not doing Combines the right way. Linda said that she did Combines all the time when she was on the sunrise shift and that she never got a write-up for making a mistake. I guess she was forewarning me. I believe they are on a track to just try and fire me. This has become ever so evident to me. Ivan and his cohorts are truly devils.

Eunice had been cleaning and set up the embossers the way I used to. I cleaned the embosser for my station and cleaned the desktop and things on it. I told Hilda that Eunice likes to do their cleaning for them. Hilda said that Eunice doesn't realize that they clean everything again anyway. Eunice is bucking to be the next D/R Supervisor. I don't really care anymore. They have already made it pretty clear that they don't want me to succeed – inside or outside of the department.

I was so tired after having worked 4 days straight. My feet and my back ached. People have no idea what you've done and what you've gone through in your life. They just feel I'm supposed to be doing the cleaning. I know that Eunice has not had the life I've had. She has a husband and not only hasn't she been working all of her life like I have, I know that she hasn't had to work nor does she have to work now. She always says that it's something to get her out of the house.

Hilda shared with me about her marriage to her ex-husband. Apparently he was a very wealthy man, but also a very crafty one who managed to get her to sign a pre-nuptial agreement. She said that they lived in Tennessee and that they were building a house and that the lot alone was worth $3.8 million. She said she had a BMW, had all kinds of jewelry, and nice clothes. She said she hired a designer who was 6-feet and blonde, and that's who is driving her BMW and living in her house today. Hilda is about 5 feet and some odd inches and brunette. I told her that hiring the woman was her second mistake and that marrying that guy was her first. She agreed. Hilda said this was why she was working two jobs. In addition to working full time at Cherokee, she was also working full-time (12-hour shifts) at the Prison. She told me how they have stores and salons in prison now. She said they live well. I told her that I needed to commit a crime and have free room and board, if it was that good.

I noticed that Tilly was listening to what I was saying. I can feel in my spirit that she is one of those who are looking for something negative to get and use against me. I remember how Louise saw me when I first came down to the Rotunda earlier. She asked how I was doing today. I know that they had been talking about me and about the write-up I received. I saw Esmerelda in the EDR when I was talking with Alma. Esmerelda never said hello or looked my way. Alma spoke to her and she acknowledged her. It's such a shame but God will have my righteousness shine as the new light and justice will prevail. In this I am confident. The enemy won't always have the upper hand and he won't last forever. Scripture tells me this and I know it to be true, by experience.

Ethel counted me out and I have zero-variance.

Chapter 35

Staff for all Seasons

August 5 – My friend in NY returned my call but we were playing phone tag; she left me a voice mail. I was so glad it was my "Friday" because it had been a long, hard week. I was so tired. I had decided to start conducting myself, at all times, down to the slightest detail, as much as possible, as if they had the surveillance cameras on me. It was in my best interest for them to do so. That way, there is always evidence of everything. This was especially true since I planned to submit a memo requesting my HR and TR employee files.

I didn't bring anything to eat or make my lunch. I didn't get as much rest I'd like to; it's hard dealing with my work hours from 2pm to 10pm on Thursdays, 6pm to 2:30am on Fridays, and 4pm to 12:30am Saturday through Monday. What makes it hard is the fact that my daughter is working days and with only one car between the two of us, I have to get up from a good sleep and take her to work. It's difficult to get the rest I need, but I'm dealing with it. Even though I tried lying down and getting more rest that day, I kept hearing this buzzing and then bell sound. I searched and tried to find it. It sounded like it was coming from the closet. I figured it must be either Sara's phone or mine but I couldn't locate either one for some reason. I searched Sara's pant pockets and didn't find anything. This went on multiple times intermittently spaced about 10 minutes apart. Finally, I was in the bathroom and heard it again. I glanced over into the trash can next to where I was sitting and there was Sara's phone. Apparently, it had fallen into the trash can. Mystery solved!

I left work earlier than usual and was determined to park on the 3rd Floor and take the service elevator, if I could find it. For some reason, my car just went into the lower lot. I came around to the Casino Floor entrance as usual. I noticed that there were 3 motor coach buses pulling in. I didn't see a TR rep. I remembered that this area closed at 4pm. The buses were apparently picking up their passengers who'd been dropped off earlier that day to play at the casino. It is so different looking at things from the eyes of an employee rather than a guest.

I had gotten to work early enough to go to Wardrobe and get the extra shirt they told me I was due because I was now full-time. I also paid about $8 and some odd cents (after taxes added) for one of the gabardine brown aprons that the dealers wear. They are pretty sturdy. The lady in Wardrobe fitted it for me and showed me that it was adjustable. I got the medium size. I had put on Sara's new pants she'd gotten. They fit me perfectly and were comfortable. Mine seem to be too big for me. I realize that I was a bit heavier when I first started working there. Sara got a larger size to accommodate her big thighs, she told me. They were still a size smaller than mine.

I saw Victoria coming down the hall but she put her head down pretending not to notice me. This is how I know when people have been talking about me. I went to clock in near HR. She was standing with a tall overweight gentleman. I waved to her but she didn't seem to acknowledge me. I remember one of the F&B (Food & Beverage) Cashier's was in front of me, along with 4 others who were waiting to clock in. Victoria and the gentleman were talking and standing off to the side but in front of me. I told the cashier that I liked their uniforms. They wore black pants and black shoes with silk-like olive green tops with a V-cut that was surrounded by a 3-pastel-colored scarf. I thought it was very becoming. She thanked me. She was on her cell phone and had a picture of a little boy. She was laughing and said, "Boys?!" I smiled and said, "Yes." Victoria allowed us to go ahead of her and the gentleman to clock in.

Ethel was in the Buzz area and I said "Good morning or good afternoon, or something" in a good-naturedly way. She made a comment and sort of laughed. Victoria came in with the gentleman. I went over and shook his hand and introduced myself. Victoria said nothing but was talking to Ethel about some event. Beverly came in and signed in. Victoria introduced him to Beverly and said, "He already met Rachel."

It was later that day while at the Rotunda that I would learn that Donald had been a cage cashier. Sara said he had too many variances and put in a transfer because he was close to being fired if he had any more variances. Sara said she'd been told he was laid back and not very fast at what he did. I told her that he would fit right in at TR. I could tell by his manner with me with he knew who I was before coming to TR.

I saw him later that day in EDR during my lunch. He was sitting with an older woman, thin, with white hair and glasses, and another younger man in a suit. Sara told me later who the woman was and that she felt she was a very nice person. I had a small salad and the Chicken Noodle Soup. The soup was pretty good. I told Brad later that evening that the soup needed Olive Oil. I shared with him how I added seasoning and Olive Oil to the Shrimp & Lobster Pasta from Brio's and put it in the oven for a few minutes.

Linda was the D/R on duty. Ethel had said Nicole would be leaving in a little while. I noticed that Arnette and Brad were talking and that Esmerelda was there also. I kept having the feeling that Esmerelda was there to spy on me. Arnette was all smiles and said hi. She was asking me about what happened and I told her that I would talk about it later. I told her that they have the cameras on me. I wasn't sure if this was the case, but I was going to assume they were. She said, "That's terrible." She was later saying that we have to pray every Tuesday and never miss a day. I agreed. I told her we were pulling down strongholds, as the Bible says.

At one point it was just Brad, Arnette, and me, then Arnette and me, then Brad and me, then Linda and me. Linda was telling me that Brad was talking about his love life. I kidded him that "Oh, that should take what . . .?" I never finished my sentence but I was insinuating that it would only take a few minutes. It's funny because Linda was kidding and telling Barbara and Beverly later that I was being mean to her. It seems innocent except people can misconstrue things. Brad said he'd been married twice. He said the first was because a mistake had been made (a baby out of marriage) and he owned up to his responsibility. He said the other was because he was bored.

Linda was asking me if I wanted to sit in the 7-Star Chair or stay in the Diamond Chair. I was going to move there when Tilly came in. I told her, "Good timing," and both Linda and I motioned for her to sit in the 7-Star Chair. It was very slow that day. I had a Black guy come in who had the same short and non-friendly attitude like the Black guy for whom I'd received a write-up. He, too, was dark-skinned and seemed unimpressed with me. However, I was determined not to give the devil any leeway whatsoever. I ignored his manner and was friendly every step of the way. He eventually came back having won a small amount from the free slot play promotion. I gave him his coupon and told him that I hoped he won a jackpot. He actually grinned a little. I think that if I had a chance to talk with the other guy we could have come to an understanding rather than blowing things so out of proportion. The only reason we didn't at that time when I was waiting on him was because neither of us was in a good frame of mind. He was not only tired and weary but he was probably disgusted and angry because he'd been losing his money. I have to always remember to be sensitive to this, especially since I've been through it myself.

Tilly's manner seemed better that evening. Barbara and Beverly were talking and seemed to have a good rapport with each other. I remembered that they were both dating (or had been dating) guys who worked at the casino in another department. The song by Denise Williams, "Let's Hear It for the Boy," came on. I noticed that both Tilly and Barbara were both singing and bobbing their heads. I said, "I'm trying to remember what movie that song was from." Both Tilly and Barbara said "Footloose!" I said, "Oh yea; however, I remember when Deneice Williams recorded it a long time ago. It's funny how sometimes they use R&B songs for movies and commercials and younger people will not know, nor care, who recorded the song, but will assume it was a non-Black person.

I made the same joke as I had made to Barbara the week before about how we all stand up when one little old lady in a walker gets in the line. She slowly makes her way all the way around and when she finally gets to the end of the line, she looks around at all of us and says, "Who wants me?" We all wave to her and she makes a decision to come to one of our stations. Then she says, "Can you tell me where the restroom is?"

Barbara had laughed more the last time I told it. Tilly commented how it was awful. She then told Beverly, Barbara and I that Mona had a little old lady that came to her counter from the 7-Star and Diamond priority line. Tilly said Mona made the old lady go to the other line. However, the old lady's son (or husband) laid heavily into Mona, shouting at her, cussing at her, and calling her names. Tilly said Mona had gone to the back and was in tears. Of course, this is all hearsay but both Beverly and Barbara commented how awful this was. We really don't know the true events. This is not to say that Tilly was not telling the truth – just her version of it.

We had gotten on the subject of having to put up with rude guests and their abuse. I told them they should be glad they work in TR because Alma had told me about dealers who've had to put up with both physical and verbal abuse. Tilly and Barbara kept saying that they don't have to put up with it, that they just choose to, and look for other people to solve their problems for them. When I mentioned that Alma told me a dealer had been spit on, Tilly said that it was illegal and that the person could report the guest for assault. I told them that I'm finding that there are a lot of things there that work in theory, but in practice they seem to be totally different. I remember Beverly asking me if I would put up with it. I told her that I wouldn't because no job is worth it.

Muriel came in later and Linda left. Eunice started cleaning again and I noticed that Tilly cleaned her station with a different countertop cleaner. While she was in the back, I cleaned my station (Diamond chair). Tilly came back out and wanted to give me the cleaner and asked if I wanted it to clean the counter. I told her that I'd already cleaned it. I told Barbara and Beverly that when I used to come in from 8pm to 4:30am I used to do a lot of the cleaning by myself. Later that morning, Linda and Morris would do the cleaning. Of course, Leslie had told me she wanted to do the cleaning when she was staying later. She said she wanted to clean the embossers and the combines because there was nothing to do.

I was extremely tired and exhausted. I know I need to work full-time but I'm so drained by the end of my work week. I hadn't noticed when Eunice was being counted out. I also believe that it was possible that Eunice and Muriel had a discussion about my write-ups. I know that something is going on but unsure as to exactly what. Beverly and I were counted out at 12:20. Ethel was there. I noticed that she'd been staying later than usual. Ethel said it was her Friday.

I had zero-variance. Sara shared with me that she'd been having zero-variance as well.

Chapter 36

Irons Sharpens Iron

August 6 – I talked with and prayed with Arnette. We both came to an agreement that our missions from God are different even though they have the same end goal: repentance and salvation through the Lord Jesus Christ. Arnette said that she was going to be delivered from her past and the past curses. I told her that I can see that it has already happened but just has to manifest itself. I know that her blessings are coming. I told her that I am God's ambassador and his tool. He uses me as he wishes. I know that I've had to suffer quite a bit in my life, but through it all, God has given me miracles, blessings, and some good times. I know that the apostles, the prophets, and many of God's messengers who had to fight battles, including the Lord Jesus when he walked the earth, did not always want to suffer what they went through, but just knowing God Almighty and his host of angels were with them, was enough to carry them through. It was their glory to suffer for Christ. Apostle Paul said that he counted all things dung but for the cross of Christ. He said he forgets the things behind him and presses forward toward the prize of the high calling in Christ.

Though I had written up some other things to be submitted to fight what I've been going through, God has shown me that wisdom is the key. I know that timing is key in everything. We searched through the Employee Manual and discovered that my 2nd write-up from the email by Bertha, could and would possibly lead to a progressive discipline. I felt that it would greatly impact my current applications and future career opportunities. Sara and I searched until we found important numbers. We called the Employee Ethics Hotline number and discovered that it was just a recording. We searched the phone numbers of the Vice Presidents/ Directors. The manual stated that we could file an incident report if we felt we were harassed, discriminated against, or experienced retaliation. We could either file a report with the Manager of Employee Relations or the VP of Human Resources. We noticed that the book did not have the Manager of Employee Relations listed. We had called and left messages with Dixie and with Alexandria but then later told them we were going to contact the Manager of Employee Relations. We found out that Bambi was the Director of Employee Relations. She is the same person who was listed as the contact when and if people had questions about the situation with Paula Deen. We were to direct questions and concerns to her. We asked and found out that Carlos is the Manager of Employee Relations. We called and left a message with Bambi. When she called back, I asked if I could make an appointment to talk with her. I told her I was very hurt by the events that occurred. She asked if I could come in at 10am on Wednesday (the next day), and I said I could.

It was a lazy day but Sara and I waited too late to go to a good place to get anything to eat. So we went to my dreaded place: McDonald's in the Food Lion Shopping Center. It's located right across from the sign you see when you're about to turn off from the 441 N Highway. There is a sign that says, "Cherokee Indian Reservation." The food there is probably the next to the worst at any McDonald's at which we've ever eaten. I was so upset that the bread was hard, the fish old (on the Filet of Fish sandwich), and the fries stale three times in a row, that I vowed never to eat there again. Of course, when you're hungry and they are the only game in town, my daughter went there anyway, and once or twice after that, I went there with her. I found myself asking them to put the meat patty on the side. Then I would come home and season it, pour olive oil on it, and then cook it in my toaster oven some more. Since that time, they have completed some very important renovations and change in management and operations.

I believe the McDonald's that gets the prize for the worst food ever is the one in Jacksonville, Florida that is near the motel that we stayed in. I had stopped eating meat again for a while because nothing tasted the same anymore. I know that they are shooting animals full of hormones. People who are younger don't really know the difference because they don't have anything with which to compare it. In fact, nothing today is as good as it was. I used to hear my parents and grandparents say these things, but, of course, you think they're saying these things because they just miss "the good old days."

People keep saying that things are getting better, but the truth is, the morals of most people are getting worse and worse every day. God tells us in his word (Bible) that this is the case. This world is so marred by sin and godlessness, that even the creation (planet) groans in agony for relief, maybe even more so than the creatures (man and animals). I know that one day God will restore everything, but in order to restore, the old has to pass away. His word says that a new heaven and new earth will come down like a bride adorned for her husband, in all her glory. The twelve tribes of Israel will judge the nations. Those of us who don't even know who we are, those of us who have stripped of our homeland in Israel (Africa), those of us who were scattered throughout all the earth because of our disobedience to God, those of us who were cursed because of this disobedience to become a byword (Black, negro, N-word, etc.), those of us who were in bondage in Egypt and put on slaves ships again in America, those of us who don't know who we really are in God – we are the ones who are the descendants of Abraham, Isaac, and Jacob. We are the ones God intended to teach and to take his word to the nations. We were supposed to be the head and not the tail. Because of our disobedience, we were the despised and the broken down. Every race of people has prospered as a group. We are the only ones who have a handful who enjoy wealth only if we can run, dance, sing, or somehow entertain the children of our former oppressors (or so I thought). However, others, especially those of European-descent, have wealth and they are not anyone famous and have no special gifts that have earned them their wealth.

Many have inherited the wealth while giving us an image. We have images in every aspect of life: those black men and women to whom we can look and give us something to which we can aspire. However, we need more than just images. We need concrete manifestation of the fruits of prosperity. If nothing else, we deserve fair and honest treatment. The nation of Israel (so-called black people) have come a long way; however, once they started to enjoy what the White men have told them was the best things in life (White women, expensive cars and jewelry, etc.), and especially when a half-White, half-Black man was elected in what is now (temporarily) the highest office in the land, they no longer felt the need to keep moving forward. What tragic symbolism accompanied the election of Barrack Obama when the two Black male commentators for BET sat back and complacently crossed their legs in triumph. I wanted to cry when I heard the young black woman exclaim, "Now the standard of beauty's going to change," (as if black women have not been the standard) and the young black boy exclaim, "We're finally going to get reparations" (still looking for the oppressor to make things right). Maybe they hadn't been listening when a white woman proclaimed, "We don't have to be afraid to vote for Obama, because he's not going to do anything for black people."

The hope of many have waxed cold; they see, after many years later where Obama has been re-elected and is now, for all intents and purposes, unless something changes (and it will), is a "lame duck." He gave the Native Americans millions of dollars for a "new start." He was instrumental in getting homosexuals the right to "get married in the sight of God." After all, he did say he was their "champion." He forced upon us all a health care plan which, in theory, will provide much needed healthcare to all, but in practice, will put us under bondage to obtain medical insurance, and will mandate us much like mandatory auto insurance. The difference is: you don't have to own and drive a car, but when your "vehicle" is your body, the only alternative is death. So, if you want to live, you will have no choice. Obama also told us to "take off our house shoes and go to work." Many of the black people who were happily employed cheered joyously and applauded his comments – that is, until they lose their jobs and find themselves trying to get a much-reduced unemployment check and signing up (online or otherwise) for a food card. So much for "walking around with bags of money," like a Black man in a Laundromat in Atlanta once told me. I remember that I hadn't bothered to respond to him after that. I knew his wake up call would come soon enough without me bursting his bubble.

Chapter 37

Can We Talk?

August 7 – Sara and I were running late and we called Bambi's office and spoke with her secretary. We told her that we would be about 10 minutes late. We got there about 10:15 am. I went through the Marketing glass door and the receptionist to whom I've seen before and had given the two thank you cards to Sam and Delilah for the interview, was the one who asked us, "Can I help you?" I told her I had an appointment with Bambi. She pointed to the other glass doors to the left outside that I never knew existed and told us that Bambi's office was through there. I thanked her and we went in. I let the receptionist know I was there. She announced me on the phone and told me to go right in. I reached out and shook Bambi's hand and introduced my daughter. I brought Sara because I wasn't about to have yet another person lie and misrepresent what I say and/or how I say it. I gave her the Incident Report and told her I wanted to file it. She asked if I would give her time to read it or did I want to tell her what happened. I said, "Oh please, take your time." I put my head down and looked at my hands until she was through reading the report. Here's the report:

DATE OF INCIDENT: Saturday, August 3

APPROXIMATE TIME: 1900 Hours

INCIDENT: Two (2) Write-Ups Based on Hearsay & Emails Resulting in Unfair and Unjust Verbal and Documented Coaching

EVENTS: I was due to take my first 15-minute break at 6p.m. but due to high customer traffic, I wasn't able to take my break until almost a quarter of 7p.m. My supervisor, Felicia, gave me the approval to take my first break. But as I was about to go, she told me she needed to have a meeting with me first. As I walked into the back office, I was surprised to see supervisor, Ethel in the room. Ethel did not say anything; she sat silently in a chair.

Felicia then presented me with two (2) emails: The first one, a second-hand account of a guest's complaint against me sent from Arnold (Cage Cashier Supervisor) and the other, from Bertha (VIP Hiring Manager). Both of these emails were sent directly to my manager, Ivan. From these two emails, I was given two (2) Performance Documentations disciplinary write-ups, the first one, a Verbal Coaching and the second, a Documented Coaching, as well as placement on the Progressive Disciplinary Ladder.

The first email, written by Arnold, described an African-American male guest who stated that an African-American female Total Rewards Representative spoke to him in a very unprofessional manner and that this rep refused to wait on him. The guest stated that he was very upset and felt that he should not have been spoken to in this manner. The guest never used my first name, last name, or badge number. He simply described an African-American female who works in Total Rewards. Without speaking to me, without getting the facts, without even verifying that I, Rachel, was the Total Rewards Rep the guest was complaining against, Arnold wrote an email directly to my manager, Ivan. Arnold could have contacted a Total Rewards supervisor who was on duty at the time, but chose not to do so. Purely taking the inaccurate information of a self-admittedly "tired and weary" guest's complaint, Arnold wrote an email to my manager, Ivan, resulting in my disciplinary write-ups, and unfair and unjust placement on the Progressive Disciplinary Ladder. This is a very serious issue, as my character and reputation, as well as my customer service and guest interaction skills have been greatly slandered.

The facts of my interaction with the African-American male guest are as follows: On July 28, guest came up to my window. I greeted the guest, like I do all the guests, with "Welcome, I'm Rachel, how can I help you?" This refutes his claim that I refused to wait on him. The guest wanted a Kiosk; he wanted to exchange his Total Reward Credits for cash. I did exactly as the guest requested, as evidenced by the $98 Kiosk I signed and printed out for him, which he then took to the cashier cage to redeem. I thanked the guest, as I do all the guests with "Thank you for coming." This refutes his claim that I was rude and unprofessional. We are taught to try and delight the guests, we are taught to try our best to energize and motivate all guests. I tried to do this with this particular guest, but he stated to me "I don't want friendly, just business." This particular guest treated me in a very rude and unfriendly way, but I still treated him in a professional, respectful, and helpful manner, even warmly thanking him when he left my window. This is an issue of hearsay, slander, and libel which has resulted in disciplinary action against me. If need be, I am requesting a full review the surveillance tapes (audio and visual) and you will have evidence that I treated this guest with the upmost respect and approached him in a friendly and appreciate manner. As such, the disciplinary write-up I received is unfair, unjust, and inaccurate and I am requesting that it be removed from my file, as well as my removal from the Progressive Disciplinary ladder.

The second email, from Bertha, was "more serious in nature" (I was told). While the first Performance Documentation had been a verbal coaching, this second one had "verbal" scratched out and "documented" hand-written on it instead. The offense was Code of Conduct #18. The email was sent from Bertha (VIP Hiring Manager) to my manager, Ivan and was dated July 30. Bertha said that I had been increasingly aggressive and rude to her. There was even capitalized letters to represent that I had shouted at her. She made comments in her email and reference to a conversation that she and I never had. In fact, the comments she made were from a phone conversation that I had with Olga in Human Resources. This is proof that they had talked about me with each other.

I was completely shocked by this email and I told Felicia that it was all a lot of "bunk." I couldn't believe what I was hearing and reading. I started to object, and Felicia told me she was "just doing her job." I told her that it was unfair to get a write-up when no one challenged whether or not Bertha was even telling the truth. Felicia said that Bertha had been at Harrah's for a long time and they'd never known her not to write something like that unless something happened. This clearly shows a bias, partiality, and conflict of interest with regards to Felicia and Bertha in this situation. I was completely hurt by the lies Bertha was writing about me in this email. I said, "Why are they doing this?" and "Well, I know why." I just shook my head and sighed. I stated to my supervisor, Felicia that I needed to have a meeting with her (Bertha) and then Felicia and Ethel Sanchez gave me two numbers of people to talk to in Employee Relations (Dixie and Alexandria). Felicia and Ethel said that I could make comments on the write-ups. I told them I wanted to put my comments in writing, so for the time being, I wrote on there "Will make comments later" on both of the Performance Documentations. Felicia said I could now go on my 15-minute break. To my surprise, Felicia made a comment that "if I wasn't coming back to let her know." I said, "Felicia, I wouldn't do that."

The facts of my phone conversation with Bertha (VIP Hiring Manager): On July 24, I called and spoke to Olga in Human Resources, as she was now in a new position conducting the "New Hires." I called Olga to find out how the hiring/application process works for internal employees applying for external and internal positions. Olga stated that "applicants meeting the minimum requirements are sent to the hiring manager, and that specific hiring manager determines who gets an interview." I had interviewed for the Sr. Account Executive Casino Host position and had applied for the VIP Host position. I asked Olga to whom I needed to speak to find out why I wasn't offered/ interviewed for a position. She stated that I would have to talk to the hiring managers. She gave me Delilah's phone number for the Sr. Account Executive Casino Host, and the phone number of Bertha for the VIP Host. I called and left a voicemail for Delilah. I then called Bertha. After identifying myself, I politely and calmly informed her that I was just trying to find out why I was not selected for an interview for the VIP Host position. She stated "I don't even know who you are." I respectfully asked her if she had seen my application and she stated she did not. I asked myself how this was possible if all applicants meeting the minimum requirements for the VIP Host position were sent over to the hiring manger.

Nevertheless, I was still respectful, kind and conducted myself in a very upbeat, positive and professional tone. This is an issue of hearsay, slander, and libel which has resulted in disciplinary action against me. If need be, I am requesting a full review of all the surveillance audio recordings of my phone conversations and/or voicemails with and to Olga, Delilah, and Bertha as full evidence and proof that I did not violate Code of Conduct #18; I conducted myself very professional at all times and showed the upmost respect toward fellow employees and especially to people who are in upper management. Why would I have an aggressive tone and speak very rudely to a hiring manager of a position to which I am applying? This is completely untrue, false, and has resulted in unfair and unjust disciplinary actions, consequently, my placement on the Progressive Disciplinary ladder.

Neither my supervisor, Felicia nor my manager, Ivan, spoke with me regarding Bertha' email before giving me a disciplinary write-up. They did not investigate her email complaint against me. They never even asked me if I had ever called and spoken to Bertha. They merely took Bertha's perception and how she viewed our phone conversation situation, and issued me Performance Documentation and a disciplinary write-up. As a direct result, I was unfairly and unjustly placed on the Progressive Disciplinary Ladder. This is a very serious issue, as my character, reputation, employee interaction skills, and respect for upper management has been severely slandered. Also, my future for career advancement with Harrah's Cherokee has been unfairly and unjustly thwarted and severely compromised. It will also seriously and negatively impact possible interviews/hiring with positions I have currently applied. This entire situation has caused me much emotional grief and turmoil. At work, I have fought back tears and still served, helped, and delighted guests with Top Box service. Not only has this caused me great emotional pain and mental anguish, it has greatly hindered my chances for promotion, raises, career advancement not only within my Total Rewards department, but especially the VIP Host department, and any human resource and management level positions.

REQUESTED ACTION TO BE TAKEN: The disciplinary write-up that I received based on Bertha' email was unfair, unjust, and inaccurate. Therefore, I am requesting that it be removed from my file. Also, I should also be removed from the Progressive Disciplinary ladder.

An injustice has been done against me. It is unfair to give me two (2) disciplinary write-ups based on hearsay. Communication is a two-way street, not solely based off what one person says about another person. I am seeking the assistance of Harrah's Cherokee Director of Human Resources to help resolve these matters, clear my name and unfairly damaged personnel file, and allow me the equal opportunity for employment advancement, honest performance evaluations, and career growth within the company.

SUBMITTED BY: Rachel, #
DATED: August 7

Sara was silent the whole time. I talked a bit about what happened. I did not want to say anything incriminating against Ivan or anyone else, but I just told the truth as the events came up in the conversation. Bambi explained the hiring process to me. She said this is how it's supposed to work and explained how they look at the applications and the 01's, then 02's and down the line. She said that if you applied for a job and it required 3 years of supervisory experience, for example, your application is not considered. She seemed surprised when I told her that I was over-qualified for every job for which I applied. She seemed surprised when I told her that Ivan said they don't give 90-day performance appraisals, only informal ones; however, I have yet to have even an informal one. She quickly told me that Bertha was correct that HR reps are the ones who tell the managers who to interview. Therefore, I was lied to by the HR rep. Even more so, it confirms that both of them were trying to "cya" and make me the fall person for investigating. Both Bertha and Olga were wrong in their treatment of me. However, I know that things go much deeper than this. I asked Bambi if the Cherokee Leader Associate position was only for . . . I never got to finish the sentence, she quickly said it was "enrollment members," meaning members of the Eastern Band of Cherokee Indians. I told her that no one told me that. Jack, who signed as the supervisor on the transfer sheet, never said a word, and Ivan, who signed as the manager, never told me either. My guess is that their practice of holding certain positions for enrollment members may not be a legal practice, especially since we are covered by Caesar's Entertainment's standards and policies and everything says Equal Employment Opportunity. I can understand that, under the Indian Preference Act of 1934, and revised under 1974, they have preference, but where does it say they can have positions where only enrollment members can apply. The problem I have with this is that I don't think this practice is legal. I also had a problem with it because I've noticed that quite a number of European-descent people are enrollment members. I truly believe there is a conspiracy against those of us who are of African-descent. I plan to call the EEOC and BIA (Bureau of Indian Affairs), anonymously of course, to find out the answers I need.

I could tell from the expression on Bambi's face, that she did not like me saying anything derogatory about Ivan and his way of doing things. She said she would get with Carlos, the Manager of Employee Relations. She said they would investigate and pull the surveillance of July 28th. She said they would try to get the phone recordings, but that it might not be possible. I asked her if it would be possible to have a meeting with Bertha with her and Carlos as mediators. She said that they don't do that because they've found it could end up in a shouting match between people. I told her that I didn't have a problem with it but that I understood. In reality, no resolution can come for me if Bertha is still allowed to be the hiring manager for the VIP Host. It would become a no-win situation for me, meaning I can never have that position. I know that this has been their plan all along. Even when you go to Employee Relations, you still lose out because you are forever more looked upon as a "troublemaker."

Arnette called and I relayed everything to her that happened. She was real apprehensive and even wrote me an email. For some reason, she thought I went to Ivan's boss. I corrected her. I still never told her the name of the person to whom I talked. Arnette is all about God giving her favor to work through the Cherokee people. In fact, she feels she will marry into the tribe. The difference is Arnette looks like the people they already accept (European-descent). They will never accept me because they too, like White people, once owned my ancestors.

Arnette is a good woman of God and she means well, but she doesn't truly understand a number of things yet. I know she'll find out pretty soon, but God will have to reveal them to her in his own time. I pray that she can accept God's word. She should see the difference even now. While Ivan told her that he would help her by introducing her to the manager for the position to which she was applying, he questioned me regarding my qualifications, told me that another person was interested in the job, and all of a sudden, I have two write-ups that were so damaging, that they will negatively impact my ability to promote to another position. I do know that God will work everything out the way it's supposed to be. I always follow his leading; however, I know that complacency is not his will for my life. There is a big difference between complacency and being content in whatever state you find yourself, as the apostle Paul stated. The difference is I am happy in Christ and give all the glory to God for his leading and wisdom for my life, whether I have abundance or whether I have little. However, "injustice anywhere is a threat to justice everywhere." We are in a spiritual battle. God has given us every weapon we need: prayer, the Word of God, faith, gifts of the Holy Spirit, and he goes before us and protects us as we sojourn through this land. We are in this world but not of this world. He gives us voice and heart. We are wise as serpents and harmless as doves. We are pulling down strongholds. We pray and then move forward in faith. The outcome and results are in God's hands. We just have to operate and move in his will, in his timing, and in his way.

I realize that Arnette and I are two different people. We don't have the same ministry or mission, but the end goal is the same. Our methods are different but it is the same God uses us. She is also led by her pastor while I am led directly by God and His word. One thing I must do is always wait for confirmation. However, I must not let fear be a determining factor. Jesus prayed three times because he wanted confirmation and wanted to know if there was any other way his mission could be accomplished without giving his life. He finally ended up saying, "Nevertheless, they will be done." I know that one day I will leave this physical earth; however, let it be in God's timing and his will be done, not mine or the enemy's. Thank you Father for your love and protection every step of the way.

Chapter 38

Taking Stock of the Situation

Sara and I drove to Asheville to the Red Lobster on Tunnel Rd. We got turned around a few times just like we did when we first came to Georgia, that is, Atlanta, but we found our way. MapQuest didn't realize that there was a new "Future West I-26" freeway. We were supposed to get off on Exit 6 from the I-26, but it was really from the I-240. We were lucky: I heard a story about a year ago where an Asian couple used MapQuest and found themselves in the ocean. For the most part, MapQuest is reliable, but of course, like anything else, you have to use wisdom and common sense.

It started to drizzle when we got there. We could hardly see the address numbers and were looking for the 139 Tunnel Rd. I noticed that there was an Olive Garden. I told Sara that Red Lobster must not be too far away because experience has taught me that, most of the time, they are located near each other since they are both owned by Darden Restaurants. I tried buying some of their stock, but it's been going down. I was hoping it would go up since they contracted with Caesar's Entertainment and the tribe to be housed in the new casino which will be located in Murphy, NC in about a year or so.

When we got there, the place was really crowded. I was surprised because it was Wednesday at 2pm. This may have been because they were located near a college campus but the majority of the people in the restaurant looked middle-aged and were mostly of European-descent. People always look at me as if they haven't seen a Black woman before. There must be something about me. I know I don't look hideous and I know I'm not considered especially beautiful according to their standards. The only thing I can think of is what my Aunt Rose used to always tell me. She said there was a light that shinned all around me, God's light. She said that I could not see the light but others could. She also said that darkness does not like nor can stand this light. This goes hand in hand with what God showed me years ago. He showed me that I could always tell what was in the heart of people by the way they treated me. Of course, I could always tell what was in them also by the fruits they bore or lack thereof.

Sara ordered for me at the bar which is where we order for take-out, while I went to the restroom. The lady at the bar was friendly and had a good sense of humor. She said it would take a "solid twenty minutes." We said we would come back. She said, smiling, that if we didn't come back when it was done she was going to eat it. I told her we'd be back in 20 minutes. Good customer service people appreciate good customer service. However, we were reminded later that the words "good," "well done," and "extra" have different meanings for different people. The lobster was large like the one in Decatur, but the bread was too doughy for my liking and I grilled the lobster a bit more in my toaster oven. Also, she had provided us with one extra small container of butter sauce. Apparently, they only give you one small container. So, two of them was extra. I told Sara that this is one of the reasons that people have some communication problems. This is why I used to give my students The Listening Test. I found that most people stop listening when they think they know what you're going to say. Also, we all have a different frame of reference and we usually think in pictures. We translate those pictures into words that we communicate to others. Others translate what they hear into their own pictures. A great number of times, we are not forming the same pictures. This is why feedback is so important. You must ask questions. You must find out if what the person intended is what we heard and translated into our own meaning. It is a constant process that takes effort.

Sometimes people seem to think alike and seem to have such good communication. So, they form relationships in some form or another. Later, they may find themselves arguing all of the time. They are dismayed and disappointed. This is especially true with married couples and they wonder what went wrong. Most of the time, while one person had one picture that represented "love and happiness," the other person had quite a different picture in mind. Ask the right questions and keep asking them and answering them before you make that commitment. This is why I believe people have to know each other longer than a "minute." We are human and prone to our emotions. It's easy to be "swept away" in passion before wisdom and common sense takes over. However, people who are led of God, pray daily, read and study their word, and with conscious effort, put on and keep on the whole armor of God, know how to "clean house" instead of being "swept away."

On our way back home, it poured rain. We had a hard time seeing a few times, that is, on the freeway. This is because other cars are driving by you and in front of our car, all the while spraying water up into the air. We made it back safely, thanks be to God. I still enjoyed my lobster and Sara had driven to Bojangles in Sylva, NC near Wal-Mart. Sad to say, the chicken was not done and did not taste good. It was a big change from the other time I bought chicken there. This had to be over two months ago. I believe, for whatever reason, the cook did not cook the chicken as long as it was supposed to be. I've been noticing that a lot of people of European-descent like their food more raw than those of us of African-descent. I know that they don't want to believe they are mutants, but everything attests to this. I also know that they really can't handle the truth about themselves. There was a college professor many years ago who had done the study into the true history of man. He said that White people would be very surprised if they knew the truth. They are of the Neanderthals. We are not. God has assured me that everything that is hidden will be revealed – everything. Also, everything that is spoken in secret will be shouted from the roof top. We cannot hide from God because he is omnipresent (everywhere), as well as omnipotent (all powerful) and omniscient (all knowing).

I play my Bejeweled-2 game each night. I have Bejeweled-3 but it's too fast-pace and annoying to me. I just want to relax. The new Bejeweled-2 game is relaxing. I'm playing the "Unending Game." I'm up to Level 53 and over one million points. I've been there before. It's strange how I can be down to just one move and eventually able to get more moves and have 3 or 4 cubes again. If anyone has ever played the game, you have moves as long as you are able to get at least 3 same-colored jewels to line up in a row or column. You can only select two of them to get this to happen, however, and once you get them to line up, they fall off and create points. When you have 4 of them, you get higher points, but the 4th one stays on the screen and becomes a highlighted item called a "power" jewel. Once you match 3 or more with it, it blows off other adjoining jewels that are not its color and shape. That is, it is powerful because it affects other groups around it. When you are able to get 5 jewels of the same color and shape in a row or column, you create a "cube." Not only do you get higher points, but a cube can be used to clear off all like shapes and sizes by clicking on it and any adjacent jewel. The game can be challenging yet not so difficult that you lose your mind. God taught me many years ago that once I learned the rules that they always apply, that is, he taught me to see patterns, shapes, and relationships in things and in life – both how they represent in the spiritual realm and have concrete manifestations in the physical realm. I've just about discovered what he's been trying to tell me. I would discover later that the principles of this game were preparing me for financial and economic success to come.

Chapter 39

Horror in Human Resources

August 8 – I dropped Sara off at work at 11am. I went to work an hour early and took in a written request to the HR Rep to provide me with copies of: The Transfer/App Form, the job description for the VIP Host position and the Cherokee Leader Associate position, and the Internal and External Job Posting for the week that would close at 4pm that day, according to the way they have been doing things. She looked at it for a long time and finally printed the job descriptions and gathered together the other forms. I noticed she went to the back and came out with another woman who looked of European-descent but was probably an enrolled member also. The woman looked at me to see who I was and what I looked like. She handed me the forms I had requested but I noticed she had not printed her name nor signed where I'd requested. I said, "Thank you very much" and showed I was appreciative.

Edna had also told me that I had to submit my resume and transcripts every time with the application/transfer because she said they didn't keep them. This is odd. I kept wondering what they did with them. Something odd is truly going on. However, I drove back home and printed out my resume and transcripts. I was losing time because HR closed at 4pm and I was due to start my shift at 2pm. Actually, because of the buzz sessions, I had to clock in by 1:53pm. I had Edward sign for the supervisor section. I asked him if I had to have Ivan sign it and he said that a manager has to sign it. This is odd because I remember when I previously applied for the VIP Host and Events and Promotions Supervisor positions that Jack had signed them and initialed for Ivan. It may have been that Ivan was not in that day. This, I don't know yet.

Since Edward had said Ivan was on a conference call and I saw that his door was closed and it had a sign on the door that said "Conference Call," I put the papers into an interoffice memo (manila) envelope and put "Time Sensitive" on it and shoved it under the door. I had asked Edward if they would either let me leave early for my break to turn it in or if they could turn it in for me. He said that they could probably turn it in for me. I kept looking at the time and hoping that Ivan would turn it in. However, I don't believe he did. I just decided it was enough right now to know that I tried.

Edward did the buzz session and there was no new information. He sent me down to the Rotunda. I notice that except for "hello" Victoria doesn't say very much. Donald was still under training but they had him on the system. Since he'd been a cage cashier before, his training time should be a lot shorter. I noticed the same Black guy who'd acted like he didn't want me to wait on him, and who had accused me of not wanting to wait on him, and accused me of being rude and unprofessional so that I received a write-up from Felicia. I was in the Diamond Chair and there was no other rep available. I said my "welcome" but he motioned his finger to Eunice (blonde-haired and white). I had wanted to wait on him to apologize if he felt I was rude and tell him that everyone is entitled not to feel well and how two people not feeling well could clash, however slightly. It may have been possible to make sure there was no future conflict, but I knew he was a coward. He'd reported me and assumed I would take things out on him. If he knew me, he'd know that this is something I'd never do. It just reminded me of how low things had become with regard to the division of Black men and Black women – a plan that was put into work a long time ago and seems to be succeeding. I think I know understand the attitude of the woman in charge of the NCNW (National Council of Negro Women). She was very adamant when it came to forever supporting Black men. She would never entertain any negative comments or criticism in this area. I believe she understood that we must never allow anyone else, however well-meaning they may be or they may seem to be, to cause division among us.

Linda was the D/R on duty and no other supervisor was down there. She told me about a cottage that she had for rent. It sounded great. It was located, she said, in Cullowhee where it was so safe that she didn't lock her doors. She said she had 3.8 acres of land and that Natasha, who used to work as D/R and is now a VIP Host, lives in one of them. Linda said it would be $600 a month and no move in cost but we would have to pay utilities. I told her I wanted my daughter and me to look at the place. She wasn't able to give me the address but she drew a map for me to show me how to get there. I worked from 2pm to 10pm. About 15 minutes after the Earth Water TR reps came downstairs, Linda sent me down to be counted out by Ethel. It was pretty slow that day. I had zero-variance.

August 9 – I dropped Sara off and went back to bed. I spent some time that day doing research, still only getting bits and pieces. I called the U.S. EEOC office and was on hold for over 40 minutes. When they finally got on the line, she gave me the number to the local office in North Carolina. She did this because I was trying to find out just to what extent the Indian Preference Act extended. I knew it included initial hires, transfers, lateral movements, and promotions. However, it seems Cherokee has been using it also for status changes such as moving from part-time to full-time, prime and/or wanted schedules and hours, and PTO. In fact, they seem to use it for almost anything when it pleases them. The only time an enrolled member may not get something, as in the case when Natasha got the VIP Host over the young man who was a cage cashier, is when the non-enrolled member has good rapport and network with the people doing the hiring or the people who are in the same position who have put in a good word, and/or if, in Natasha's case, the person has more education than the enrolled person. In my case, because I am a Black woman, it doesn't seem to matter. They don't want me in there. I know it is the enemy who is really trying to keep me out.

Chapter 40

Just Call Me Toby

It was pretty busy as usual on a Friday evening. I still have to work 6pm to 2:30am. I saw the same Black guy who reported me unfairly and caused me to receive a write-up. Again, I was the only person open. I tried to welcome him and he pointed to Beverly and went to her. How embarrassing to have someone who is supposed to be your protector and covering (in general as a Black man) to choose anyone else of another race other than you, for whatever reason. Of course this happened at the Rotunda. I wish he'd go up to Earth Water instead.

I left messages for North Carolina EEOC and will call them back if I don't hear from them on Monday. I talked to Reese for some length of time. I had to correct the chapter in Deuteronomy that I'd given him that tells about Black people being Hebrew Israelites and the curse we were under because of our ancestors' disobedience. We should have had the blessings, but disobedience comes with a very high price. It was Deut. 28. He's also going to get the DVD "Hebrew or So-Called Negro." I think he's finally starting to understand. We talked about the enemy's plan to use the people of European-descent to divide and conquer God's true and original people.

When I came in at 6pm, Beverly and Victoria had already been there for 4 hours. They were working 10 hours that day. So far, I haven't been scheduled for a 10-hour day. During Buzz, Eunice was commenting that some of the reps haven't been explaining the Hidden Jackpot promotion fully to guests and that she was finding that a great number of Diamond and 7-Star Players did not know about the promotion. Ethel also read an email from Ivan where he was giving an analogy about his garden and how he had to rid himself of the weeds in order to have a better looking garden. In others words, Ethel said, we needed to get to the root of the problem. In my spirit, I knew Ivan, in light of my incident report, was referring to me as a troublemaker and insinuating that when I left, all would be well. This was further emphasized by the fact that Ethel said our FH (Friend/Helpful) scores were down and our WT (Wait Time) scores were up. She said that the FH scores being down had never been heard of before. Where before we were told to cut down on our spiel so we could speed up our process, now it was suggested that we focus only on one promotion at a time and spend more time giving the guest more information. This was a good idea; however, I came to the defense of our reps. I said that for the most part we have very good reps. I said I also found out that the scores we receive are based on surveys taken way after the fact. Most people usually only remember the very last experience they had. Even if they had positive experiences before, if they lost their money, this can usually color their attitude about their experience. The TR rep may have been friendly and helpful, but sometimes they see us as people who are agents just to get them to invest/lose their money in the slots and the tables. Never mind that we never twist their arms to make them place bets or put money into the slots. The casino is a business just like others. Despite any influence, marketing, or advertising, each person has a choice.

TR Reps, Table Games Dealers, Cage Cashiers, VIP Hosts, Sr. Acct. Executive Casino Hosts, Gaming Hosts – we are all the front line people, just like the military. The difference is we're sent to the front lines in battle with only our smiles, our customer service skills, our wits, and our training. However, we have no defense weapons. To a great extent, that even some of the naïve reps know, we must take a great deal of abuse. The nature of gambling itself puts us in this awkward position. This, coupled with the fact that Cherokee is the only casino in North Carolina, Georgia, Tennessee, Virginia, and South Carolina, gives them a monopoly. Commerce was originally designed to prevent monopolies. However, people love playing the game of Monopoly. It feeds into the greed and control of the un-regenerated human spirit. It's a "winner, take all" mentality.The world of gambling emphasizes and enhances this way of thinking. So, it is greed, control, and vanity. Let me be the only one who has all the marbles/chips. This means I am the best and gives me a sense of control. Now I am somebody because I can buy and sell just about everyone and everything. The Devil tried to tempt Jesus this way, but our Lord and Savior in all his wisdom said, "It is written, man shall not live by bread alone, but by every word that proceeds out of the mouth of God," "You shall not temp the Lord our God," and "Get behind me, Satan, you shall serve the Lord our God and him only shall you serve." Only a heart that is truly touched by God's grace can have compassion on others instead of thinking only of one's self and even giving out of selfish interests.

Ethel also pointed to an envelope with voting slips in front of it where we were supposed to vote for our department representative to be a Manager Review Board. I'm not sure if this is something they have done before or if it something they are doing now in light of my recent meeting with Bambi and filing the incident report. Ethel said the board would review and determine whether a challenged disciplinary write-up would stand or if a termination should stand. However, the representative for whom you vote had to be someone who had been there at least 90 days. Here's the clincher: the person had to have been full-time status for 90 days. Can they scream any louder, "Rachel, we don't want you on the board!" To-date, I've been there close to five months.

A strange event occurred today. A young Asian guy who was in business casual attire, came up to my counter. I know he picked me out specifically because he could have gone to the other counters. He first said he wanted to get a room and said that he knew I could get him a room. I offered to take him down to the black public phone so he could call the front desk. I noticed he held his Gold TR card in his hand for me to see that it was a God card. After much garbage talk, I realized he was either a "shopper" as they sometimes use people to do external spotlights on you, or just a wise guy kid. I got his ID and looked up his account. He commented that if he was a Diamond or 7-Star player, then I would be able to get him a room. I told him that I was unable to do anything except get information for him. Everything I offered or presented to him, he would either discount or say that he already knew about it or checked with them. When I mentioned that if he had a representative, I could then get a VIP Host to talk to him, and that maybe they could do something for him that I couldn't. His interest piqued and he asked me about the VIP Host position. I told him that he could go to HR on Monday. He interrupted me before I could finish and wanted me to tell him what a VIP Host does. Then he said he was more interested in getting a room than he was learning about the VIP Host position. I just told him that the employment was not my expertise in my position but that an HR person could help him better on Monday.

He then turned the conversation to personal. He asked me how old I was because he said that age was an attitude. I told him I was 103 since age was a state of mind, as he said. He said his mom was 52 and that he keeps trying to tell her that she's not too old. He said his mom was an immigrant, didn't speak English, and came over to America with two small children. He was proud of what she had accomplished. He showed me a picture of himself where he was a bit thinner and looked scraggly and older. He proudly commented that this was him just a year ago and that I should look at him now (and be impressed, of course). I told him that the world today had "gone to the dogs." He frowned and said that if that was the case, we should just throw all of the babies in the ocean. I said not so, because our lives don't belong to us. He said that he was depressed and that maybe I needed therapy. I told him that I was quite content. I told him that I my life was not own and that I was bought for and paid for with a price, that is, by my Lord Jesus Christ. I told him that I have hope because there will be a new heaven and a new earth and that I live my life day to day and enjoy what I can until that day. He commented that he was a Christian in the 22 years that he's been alive. I told him to just keep living and he would soon understand. He said that he talked to 5 security guards and I was the first one who gave him the type of responses I did. I watched him leave and I knew that I would probably hear about this conversation later during HR and Employee Relations "investigation."

Chapter 41

I Park Therefore I Am

August 10 – Friday and today (Saturday) are my hardest days. Notwithstanding I'm working during the Sabbath (Friday evening to Saturday evening), it's also hard on me because after getting off work at 2:30 am on Friday, I have to get up and take Sara to work 7-8 hours later and then it's difficult to get back to sleep. Then, I also have to come to work at 4pm. It's not as easy for me as it was when Sara was dropping me off at work. I know that I should have stuck to my original plan and not park in the lower level anymore but I was very concerned about Sara being able to find the car and about her safety. In addition to all of this, it rained today. So, I parked on the lower level because I was running out of time and did not want to be late. It's good that things happen the way they do even when it seems detrimental to me because I always learn something and get more information about people and myself in the process.

I was quiet and Linda commented on it. I told her I only speak when I have something to say. Eunice is funny; she talks quite a bit about her home life and other things. I just listen when she's talking to others, but mostly, I tune out. After Ethel had given me my coupons, it was just she and Linda and I in the Buzz area. I had just signed the acknowledgment sheet that I received the coupons (10 $50's, 25 20's, and 75 $5) totaling $1,375. We got an extra 25 five-dollar bills because it's been high volume on Saturdays and reps had been running out of 5's. I said, "Wake up, Rachel." It was then that the enemy knew I was in a weak and vulnerable state. I was flanked on both sides: Linda on my left and Ethel on my right. Ethel said, "Rachel, can I ask you a question? Have you been parking on the first floor?" I looked at her and said, "Yes, I did." She then told me that we are not to park on the first floor ever but on Saturdays we're supposed to be parking in the lower lot. I said, "That's not the lower lot"; however, the reflection in my voice presented it as a question rather than a statement of fact. She sort of gave a wry smile and said, "No, that's not." We both knew that I knew better. However, I was determined not to lie. Fran, the D/R had come in and was signing out. I said that I thought that if we came in later, like 4 or 6pm, that it did not apply. I really thought the no parking in the casino was just because of the time they wanted us to take the bus ride from the high school; however, this was only for the high days. Ethel told me that employees are supposed to park on the 5th Floor and above. Now, this is something I really wasn't aware of. I thought we could park on the 3rd Floor as long as it was toward the back. Sometimes we do what we see others do and follow suit, sometimes we do what we hear co-workers saying we're supposed to do, and sometimes we just do what we want to do.

The truth is I didn't really want to know exactly where to park, so I could just park down on the lower level and make it easier for my daughter and me. Ethel said the lower level was just for managers. Linda added later when Ethel wasn't there that it was also for supervisors. I deduced that D/R workers could park there when they were on duty as supervisors and could not when they were in uniform as front line workers. I now realize that the person who designed the whole work system must have been someone who had been in the military. Everything they do is fashioned after the military – something for which I really have no respect anymore. You don't question authority; you shut up, obey orders, and do as you're told. All of the time is written in military time. It was the same way when I worked at Northrop Corporation (now Northrop-Grumman). I'm finally beginning to understand. It's so strange, because you have this old archaic system of autocracy in a world that is supposed to be democratic with an increasing workforce of younger people who are given positions and high ranking but still comparatively very little money. I was drafted when I wasn't looking! However, I would learn later that the situation was even worse: I didn't know I was still a slave.

I felt uneasy after that encounter with Ethel but I prayed silently and shook it off. I knew that I would be getting another write-up. Even if no write-up came, it would still be in my employee file. My daughter came by the Rotunda earlier and I told her what was said about the parking. I told her that the car is down on the lower level right now but we would have to park on the 5th Floor after that. She knew I was talking for the surveillance and recordings rather than to her. She understood and played along. I was determined that we would have to walk circumspectly, but we are still so very human.

Chapter 42

Down, I Mean Up To Earth Water

Felicia came in later. Natasha was helping someone and was being waited on a rep to my left. It was very busy that day. Because people were being waited on by a rep next to me, the person in the general line couldn't see me. Natasha motioned to them to come over. She said, "Sorry, I'm just so used to doing that." I could tell that she sort of missed working in that capacity like she used to. Also, she's no longer a supervisor. I know she gets much more money but she's lost her status. Also, I'm surprised that she's still working when she has to be about 7 months pregnant.

Apparently someone was leaving from Earth Water TR and Ethel asked Felicia to send someone upstairs. Felicia looked at Beverly and me and said, "So, should we flip a coin to see who's going upstairs." I asked her if she wanted me to go. I told her I'd go upstairs if she wanted me to do. She consented and I went up to Earth Water. It was even busier than the Rotunda. A lot of people get off the elevators and come straight there and many of them are staying at the hotel and therefore, go to the 2nd Floor where the casino is, even though they still have to take the escalator down to the casino floor where the gaming area is. So, the first thing they see is Total Rewards. They don't know that I don't mind working on the 2nd Floor. It's a job any way you look at it. I'm sure Ethel was surprised to see me. I sat at the computer down at the end where the rope was sectioned off. I asked the person to my left, who was not a rep, if I could borrow the blue VOID stamp. I then noticed that she was in business casual. I also noticed a long-haired dirty blonde woman who I realized was Delilah, with whom I had interviewed for the Sr. Account Exec. Casino Host position. I then realized that she had noticed me before I noticed her. There was another young man in a suit with her also. All three of them were of European-descent. I also discovered later when my daughter told me, that there are 3 more internal positions for the Sr. Acct. Exec. Casino Host posted on the wall in HR. Not only has Delilah not returned my call since a month ago, but she did not have the common decency to even acknowledge me. They are devils the whole lot of them!

At first I didn't move down when there was a computer open next to me because I liked where I was working. Ethel didn't say anything about it. However, when Barbara came back from her break, she took a computer to my right. Ethel came and told her to move down to the 7-Star seat when the other person who had been there left. I'm not sure if they're aware of it or not, but I no longer care about sitting in the 7-Star and/or Diamond Chair. I just like being at a computer that works. I get all kinds of different players either way. It seems as though the computers at the Earth Water TR are in a little better condition than the ones at the Rotunda. The SmartTop for the units we use to scan the ID's seems to work more often than not as opposed to those at the Rotunda. However, you only have to press the CNTRL + ALT + Delete button and bring up the task bar. Then "end process" for the SmartTop and double-click on the desktop icon to restart it. Sometimes pressing F1 to go back out of the page and typing "10" to get back in, will resolve the problem. There are times when unplugging the cable, waiting 30 seconds, and plugging it back in, will work also.

I did my job as usual and waited on everyone like I was supposed to. I tried to make sure I gave them as much information about the hidden jackpot promotion as possible. I noticed that as the day was approaching, people were becoming more excited about it, whereas, back in July, it was more "ho hum, another promotion – big deal."

I had one guest who could only talk in a raspy whisper. His eyes were glassy and sullen, and he was sort of bent over. I could tell he was not well. It was sort of ironic because when I called up his account it came up White Rd but his driver's license said Black St. I called out the street to verify if that was his account and he said he never lived at that address. I then waited a couple of minutes and then turned because I was going to get Ethel. To my astonishment, but not really surprising, she was already standing nearby observing me. She came over when it looked like I needed help. I told her what was going on. She asked him about the address and he whispered what he'd told me. Then, she went a step further and asked if he had lived in the city in North Carolina. He said he did. So, she told me to just update his address. I notice that no phone number was on his account and asked for his number. He started whispering it. I then gave him a pen and paper and told him to please write it because I didn't want him to strain his voice.

I keep wondering about people like him. We have people come in who are in wheelchairs, people who can barely walk, people who can barely talk, people who can barely hear, people who can barely breathe, people who can barely see, and people who spend their last day alive at the casino. Some people are wheelchair bound and can barely move anything except their hands. Their hands are all they need. They can just sit there and push buttons and watch the slot machine wheels roll round and round. They are entertained without moving a muscle on their body. Entertainment makes us forget about our problems and cares in life. It takes us away for a time but when we get back, everything we left is still there. So, the casino does provide an outlet like other hospitality/entertainment establishments. It is the people who participate in the games who have to budget and balance their money and their time. It is the responsibility of the people that comes into play. If you're not prepared to win or lose a specified amount, then you shouldn't play. Most people don't plan. We see it every day when they don't have their TR card and/or coupons because they were either "passing through" or just decided to drop in on the "spur of the moment." Some even want to know if we have any rooms available because either they've decided to spend the night so they can keep gambling the next day and they're too many miles away from home, or they're too drunk to drive home.

There was one amusing event with a Black couple (male and female). Barbara was waiting on the female and I was waiting on the male. The guy asked me if they still have the Russian Roulette tables. I giggled and told him that we make a point not to have Russian Roulette tables. He laughed and realized his mistake. He said he meant Roulette tables. Barbara also laughed. Linda and Ethel were standing to the right of me. Ethel was talking to Linda about something and holding a spreadsheet. I turned and told them that our guest wants to know if we have the Russian Roulette tables. They laughed also but I could feel Ethel's spirit that she did not really enjoy me being there and did not enjoy me being in a good frame of mind. So, Satan, deal with it!

This was the day that Jack was bringing in and cooking his two 100-pound pigs, as they put it. When I was asked about it, I said I would not partake because of my high blood pressure. When I mentioned this to Jack toward the end of my shift, he said there was chicken in there also. I heard others throughout the day commenting how they were so full, how good it was, and how people from other departments were saying what a good time they had. I did go up to the 2nd Floor to see if there was anything I could eat. I noticed that they had a sign that said, "Total Rewards/Valet and Promotions." It was then that it was confirmed that Ivan and the rest of the managers for all the positions for which I applied were all in cahoots. None of them want this little old Black woman to move upward and/or forward. I know that I have to allow God to use me even though I may not reap the total rewards and success of my battle. Sometimes we have to allow God work out what he wants to work out in us, for us, and in spite of us. At first I thought it was the room where the sign was but when I looked in there, there was no food or any plates, etc. I noticed an open door down the hall and went in there. There were paper plates and cups and napkins. I noticed several pies. I saw the big ovens that they use in restaurants in there. I opened both doors one at a time and saw trays of shredded meats. I saw beans and macaroni and other things that I didn't recognize. For me it wasn't very appetizing. In fact, the place had been left pretty messy. I knew though, that the EEC team would be cleaning it up later. I knew that Jack and others had probably put a lot of work into the planning and preparing of the foods and festivities. Also, I knew that Jack must have worked on his day off because he was in casual street clothes.

Since Earth Water TR closed at 12pm on Saturday and it was about 11:50pm, things had slowed a bit. Ethel had to make a decision as to whom she could let go a bit early. She said, "Why don't we let Rachel go?" They all agreed. As I was leaving, I commented and smiled, "I'd like to thank everyone who voted for me." Linda smiled but then had a serious look on her face. I could tell her mind went to the Manager Review Board ballots and how I was a person, as well as she, for whom no one could vote.

If anyone was qualified to be on that board, it was me. I not only served on several boards including an executive board, but also the workforce development board in Pinal County and created an advisory committee on which I presided. I was invited to be a mediator for the State of Arizona and provided with free training. I attended one session. This was on September 2, 2001. The following week the session was cancelled due to that dreadful and ill-fated event on September 9, 2001 ("9-11"). I was so distraught over the event that I did not continue my training. I knew that our government was behind this catastrophe. I knew they had perpetrated lies and deceit and had caused so many people, victims and attempted rescuers, to lose their lives. There was only one great mediator that was needed; that was God. Any issues over which I could preside would be minor and trivial compared to the larger scheme of things. So, all in all – among many other qualifications, I was the most qualified, but from what I've seen in this industry and many others, this doesn't mean a hill of beans when you look like me. I also know that my religious beliefs and the fact that I stand for God's way according to the Bible, and not man's way which says "anything goes," is another discouraging factor for those, like many in this industry, whose morals leave a lot to be desired – and that's putting it mildly. I've never seen so many homosexuals except those who were covert in church and those who were overt at pep rallies and the first time I went to San Francisco. It amazes me how homosexuals claim they are the underclass and are discriminated against and try to align themselves with the civil rights movement. This is a joke! Many of them, especially those of European-descent, can get jobs we cannot. They are higher paid than many of us and they are promoted faster than any of us. When I say "us," I mean Black people in general, Black women in less general terms, older Black people more specifically, older Black women even more specifically, and finally, Black people (young and old, male and female) who are totally committed to God.

Now many will read this and wrinkle their self-righteous brows and say that I should never be working in this industry in the first place. I have always gone and had to be where God placed me, regardless of the circumstances, and regardless of whether I wanted to be there or not. However, I'm very well aware that my actions, circumstances, and consequences had a great deal to do with my predicament. Sometimes God wants to teach us something that we don't quite understand until later. As long as we're obedient, all is well even when it doesn't feel well.

Chapter 43

Au Contraire, Mon Frere

August 11 – I've been slowly working on marketing my books (again). This time I am determined to get them into bookstores. I decided to focus on the Christian market. I found one Christian bookstore that I'm targeting. I researched and found their website. I talked to a store manager who said I would have to send an email to their new products email address. I provided a link to The Last Visitor, Being a Well Body of Believers, Spiritual Cosmetics for the Soul for Men & Women, and This Hill I Climb. I gave the links from Createspace. I went on Bowker to update FM Publishing Co. information with new address and phone number. I've wanted so much to get back to the nonprofit end. I've wanted to research and approach the tribe with a plan for a GED/Adult Education program and use the empty Soco Motel. I keep thinking how it would make great classrooms. I know that it would have to be cleaned and fumigated because I've heard it was roach-filled. Maybe this is why it's empty. I will just keep praying and let God open and close the doors. Right now I'm focused on promoting my books. God make a way for me, please.

I told Ethel that evening in buzz that I had parked on the 5th Floor. She didn't say anything because there was no one else in the room. She, like my daughter and I, and probably others, are making sure another person is in the room to verify what we say and how we say it. Victoria, Eunice, Barbara, and Linda came in a few minutes later. I had come through the Buzz area early and went to clock in the back area where kitchen workers clock in. I was right on time at 3:53pm. Victoria sat facing away from me. I can read body language very well. I could also feel her spirit. Her manner told me that she wanted Ethel and anyone else to know that she was not with me or for me in anyway. Unfortunately, I perceive her to be another devil. I remember her commenting that the people in the other departments were raving about how good the cookout was. She said that if someone could "stick a pin" in her and let the gas out, she would love it. I was trying to be light-hearted and said, "Would you please do that in your own designated area?" She said, "No, no," and then others tried to make it light. She said something about "my space" and made motions with her hands around her. Despite it all, they think this really bothers me. I'm used to others being against me. They don't realize that as much as I have love for my fellow man, their opinions don't count. It is only God who I am trying my best to please. None of them have a heaven or hell to put me in, but he does, as they will all soon see.

There was not much Buzz information. Ethel asked Victoria about Donald and how he was doing. She said that he's catching on really quickly. When I went down to the Rotunda, I noticed that he had signed in early. Apparently he had cone in either at 1pm or 2pm. I saw Arnette there. She told me she had an interview for the position she had been seeking. I told her that it was good. When she asked about my interview, I told her I never got an interview except the one for the Sr. Acct. Exec. Casino Host position. I told her that I had applied again for the VIP Host. I told her I would keep applying. She said, "Yeah, just keep applying." I'm only doing it for "GP" (General Purposes) because they never intend to give me a break. I told her that it must be nice for Donald to be the last one hired and already getting earlier hours than me and others. She didn't say very much. I could tell by what she didn't say, that her attitude toward Ivan is not the same as mine because he's helping her. I'm sure she'll get the position. Just as much as I'm sure he put a good word in for her, I'm sure he put in a negative word for me. I can't prove any of these things, but the devil cannot hide for too long. I'm sure he'll rear his ugly head on Monday.

Poindexter, once again, had his receipts lying on the computer. They said he went to either the restroom or the Motor Coach area and would be back in a few. I had wanted to move down but I did not want to touch his receipts. Mona came over and put them in his chair. She also commented later how a guy had gotten really upset with her because she told him he had to go to the other line and that the front line of the 7-Star and Diamond was a priority line for those players. She said the guy was rude and told her, "Sorry, if I inconvenienced you!" Her version and outlook of the event was different from that of Tilly's account. Only a recording and recap of the surveillance could tell what actually and specifically occurred and what was said.

I noticed that Poindexter kept touching Arnette and/or coming close to her face. She seemed to just deal with it, but when I started noticing it, he seemed to back off a bit. I need to ask her about it later because he could be verging on sexual harassment. When one of my guests came up and asked how the TR card worked, I started explaining to them about their reward credits, how they are calculated, how they are used, and then started to explain about the Tier Score. I first told them about the amount needed to be a Platinum card holder and what it meant. Poindexter interrupted by saying, "And what if they had 20,000 Tier Score?" I said kindly but also matter-of-factly, "Please don't interrupt when I'm with a guest." I then went on to say, "As I was saying before I was so rudely interrupted . . ." I noticed that Poindexter had his head down and was counting his coupons and receipts. Earlier, before this incident, he said he ran out of coupons and needed a loan. I asked him how many he needed. He said 4 $5's would do it. I told him to give me an IOU. He wrote it and I gave him the $5's. Later, when Lance came in, I told him about the transaction. He kind of smiled and said, "You got an IOU from Poindexter." However, later, Poindexter came back and gave me 4 of his receipts. I then tore up the IOU.

Chapter 44

Black is an Attitude?

A guest came back for the 3rd time. Eunice had helped the man's wife with a Play & Stay and issued her the $75 in coupons. There was some confusion with the husband because he said he and his wife both had rooms booked because they had other family members with them. So, they had two rooms. Eunice had gone on break and he said she had been trying to get it settled but hadn't heard back yet. I called for him and finally got an account number as verification. I won't issue the Stay & Play unless they are on the list and/or I add them after receiving the account number. The rep from the front desk said that the couple had booked the two rooms the "wrong way." However, later Lance received a call from Vera who was the supervisor of the VIP Host call center. I know this because one of the other reps took the call and announced it to Lance. Apparently, the husband was not due the Stay & Play offer. Lance said that Vera said they would write it as a loss on their end. He told me it was smart of me to get a confirmation number as a CYA. I told him that I always do that because I didn't want to get a $75 variance.

It occurred to me that this Vera must be the same Vera who had sent an email to Ethel which was forwarded to Felicia about my "tone" and my being "frantic" over the phone about a month earlier. It's interesting that she's the supervisor of the VIP Host call center. This was after I had applied for the VIP Host position. It's becoming quite clear how they are all such demonic beasts. I'm grateful because I've prayed to God that everything done in secret be brought to the light, and that everything whispered in the ear be shouted from the rooftops. He's slowly but surely bringing these things to pass.

I remember one guest I was waiting on had received a bungee cord from me. We now had the cords back. Lance was the supervisor on duty until later when Muriel would come in, but at that time he had on his suit. He was beside me waiting on a guest and when the guest asked for a cord, he said we were out of them momentarily. The guest looked at me and started to say something because they had seen me give one to my guest. I whispered to Lance that we now had the bungee cords. He apologized to the guest and said that he was glad I was keeping him on his toes. I said that he had been gone and we had just got them today. Afterwards, I told him I didn't want to interrupt and explained that his guest saw my guest with one. He said it was okay and he was glad I told him.

It was lighthearted down there and Lance and I were kidding Barbara about taking her breaks. It was good synergy. Hilda and I were talking about how there must be a better way to make a living. I remember she said she used to make $2,000 a week and travelled quite a bit. I also remember a trashy-looking and odd-shaped blonde woman of European-descent with a white top hanging to one side and shorts and pumps came up to Hilda's window. After Hilda waited on her, Hilda commented to me that the woman looked exactly how the woman looked for whom her ex-husband threw her (Hilda) over. Hilda said that the next one was going to be gorgeous, meaning her next husband. I told her that I'm praying for that to happen to her and that he be "stinking rich." I should have told her though that I hope he's a man of God who will love her unconditionally. This is the kind of "rich" I am praying for. I want him to be rich in spirit and love for others, especially her and God.

I had a couple, a thin blonde woman and heavier set man (both of European-descent) come to my counter. Both of them were drunk. It was the man's birthday. I had stopped singing happy birthday. I only join in if someone else announces it. They were both sloppy and disgusting. I say this because of their conversation. I could tell they were racist. He kept saying that she, meaning his girlfriend, had some Obama in her. He said it twice and I commented that probably Obama had some of her in him, meaning he was half-White. I think the guy meant something sexual, but I didn't take it that way at the time. He was talking about her having a big butt. I couldn't tell but she was pretty thin. She said that women take it a different way. She asked me what I would think if someone told me that. I said that I would think they were saying that I was overweight. He said it was not an insult and that saying she had a fat a** was a compliment. After I told them about the promotions, he was saying if he won the cash or the million dollars they were both coming back and taking me to dinner. I kind of shrugged and said, "No thank you." I told him that I can't take anything. He said it didn't matter that they would anyway. He then read the look on my face and said, "Oh, you don't get into that, huh?" I was so glad when they left and told Arnette so. I had to rebuke the enemy right then and there. I realize that I'm a fish out of water working in that place. I know God will give me my reprieve when I've finally learned my lesson and fulfilled my duty there.

It is such a difference in the Black people that come through there compared to the White people. I find a few of the little old ladies who are White who are pleasant and with class; even most of the young ones are fine – probably because everything is new to most of them. Oh, but the middle-aged ones who are drinking! I know these people are hurting, even those who have money, but they don't know they need the Lord in their lives. God help me find a way to reach them in your way and in your time. I am limited in my present capacity. Help me reach them. You alone are wise and have all the answers. I leave the "how" in your loving hands.

I saw the Black lady who is a table games dealer who told me to tell my daughter to stay in the Cage because some days she (Sara) makes more than she (the dealer) does. I talked with her in the hall outside of the EDR just briefly about what I'd gone through. I think she misunderstood about what I meant by my degrees. She said that it didn't matter because you didn't need one to work at the casino. She said that she was hired as a supervisor of the table games but she didn't want to work in that capacity because she could make more dealing. I told her that yes, she had been hired from the outside as a supervisor, but that no Black woman in that whole place has ever been promoted from within to a manager level. She commented that there was a Black man who was a manager. I didn't hear the name she was using because I saw Victoria come down the hall. I moved to the side to tell her that I didn't want the person I worked with to hear me. When Victoria passed by, the Black woman told me that she was 68 years old. I couldn't believe it. Even Sara thought she was probably fifty-something. The woman said that she gets $1600 a month from retirement on top of what she makes as a dealer. She said that I should go to Employee Relations about my issues and I told her that I had. She said she needed to talk to someone because she's been asking for better hours and needed them because she has an invalid son at home.

I saw Luis dressed in a uniform. I told him I hadn't heard from Pablo but that I had sent him an email. I told him that I had filed an Incident Report with Employee Relations. He told me that it was good I had done that. It's interesting how there is a glimmer of hope the Black people like Luis, Alma, and others have; however, I wonder how many of them will stand up and be counted for when push comes to shove. I pray that God work it all out. By the time Muriel came in and I was waiting on my last few guests, my hands were so cramped and weak, along with the rest of my body that ached. However, I know this is nothing compared to what my ancestors had to go through. I can stand this as long as God says.

Linda counted Eunice out and it looks like there was a discrepancy. While they were working it out, I went back to the Security area and clocked out. I then went to the EDR to get a knife and fork. Someone made a coconut and lemon meringue pie that was sitting on the counter in the Buzz area. It sure was good. I think Tilly may have made it. I got two pieces. My intent was to give one to Sara but she didn't want any and I ate all of it at home.

I had zero-variance. I believe Sunday is the calm before the storm that it is to come. God help me to weather through.

Chapter 45

Deception Interception

August 12 – I got a call from Phoebe in HR around 10am. She asked if I was still interested in the VIP Host position. My guess is there were no 01, 02, or 03 who applied and met the minimum qualifications. I was told I was listed as an "04." I told her I was still interested and she said "they" were interviewing in the HR Dept. at 10am on Tuesday. Sometimes what we think is a great opportunity can be very deceiving. This is why God deals with me in the way he does and I listen for his cues, his word, and his providence. At first I thought this was great. I already had the position in my mind. I started formulating what I would say in the interview. Sara told me that an enrolled member, who was a cage cashier and had been interviewed but did not get hired, had been asked: "What would you do if it was slow on the casino floor?" I told her that I would probably walk around and ask guests how they were doing, whether or not they were enjoying their stay there, and if they had any suggestions as to how we could improve our service and/or operations to make their experience more pleasurable. I was looking forward to the interview. I knew we had seen Ross Dress for Less at the Mall over in Asheville not far from the Red Lobster (our new landmark). My goal was to find an outfit there.

I dropped Sara off from work and noticed that I had less than ½ tank of gas. I stopped at Exxon and pretty much filled up the tank. I thought my trip would be just as effortless and straightforward as it had been the two times Sara and I had driven there. Wrong! I took the 74-East route rather than the 19-North, even though the 74-W route was longer. The 19-North takes you around the mountains and there were so many twists and turns that it actually takes you longer (or so it seems). It's more of a cumbersome trip. Besides, Sara and I had made the trip with no problems.

I made it to Asheville with no problem. My route called for taking the 74-E to the 40-E to the 240-E and then staying on the 240-Expressway to Exit 6. Total trip was about 50 miles, about an hour and 15 minutes, that is, for those of us who drive the speed limit. For some reason, I could not find the Ross store. I don't know if it was because I didn't have anything to eat or what, but my mind was not working well that day. I ended up finding a K-Mart. Actually, the sign I first saw said K-Mart Pharmacy. Of course, my mind went immediately back to Dustin Hoffman's Idiot-Savant character in Rain Main who said, "K-Mart sucks." So, I kept driving and went over to the Mall. I saw Dillard's and had remembered the one time I'd visited that store in Arizona. Even though I've found the cost of living in North Carolina a bit less expensive than Arizona, I did not want to pay Dillard's higher prices. Somehow I found my way to JC Penney. I went in around the way where the trucks go because I wasn't sure where to go. There were only 4 cars parked in front. It was pretty deserted in there. When I went in the front entrance I saw clothing and items for men only. I asked someone whether or not the women's apparel was on another floor and the woman said "It must be." I saw escalators only, no elevators. I took the escalator going down and saw children's clothing. There were "back to school sale" signs everywhere. I saw and heard a few families with their kids walking through the store. I finally found the women's apparel. I found dress slacks that were grey, some were dark blue, and some that were black. I also found blazers that were dark blue and some that were black. I took both a size 12 and a size 14 which I thought were black pants and size 14 of the black blazers. I searched and found a fuschia-colored top and a garden-green top. Both were simple, cotton tops with short sleeves and buttoned up to the top with a simple round collar. I chose the green top and went into the dressing room to try them on. There were only two rooms and a lady was waiting outside holding a few garments. Apparently she was waiting for the person she was with who was trying on clothes. The size 12 fit but they were really fitting. It wasn't that they were too tight but I had to remember that I was dressing for an interview and not a date. The size 14 was not too large and I felt more comfortable in them. The blazer was a large size and fit fine. I had wanted the short blazer but, once again, my behind, as most black women, was a big prominent. Even though I had tried on the grey slacks, I decided to get the black pants and the longer black blazer. I felt this would go better with my dark brown skin off-set by the green top. My mind went back to how stylish Steve Harvey looked in his black and winter green the last time I saw him on Family Feud. However, the black pants did not look exactly the same color as the black blazer. I had to really look at them. Then I noticed that the pants were actually a real dark blue, not black. I went and exchanged them. They now matched the jacket. I went to pay for the items and remembered that I needed stockings and earrings.

 The saleslady was nice and suggested I could get 20% off by applying for a JC Penney charge card. I was excited about the possibility; the credit card company wasn't. I had told the saleslady I was pushed for time because I worked for the casino in Cherokee and had to get to work before 4pm. She hurried as fast as she could. She very nicely said, "It didn't go through, but wait a couple of months and you can try again." This was so much more tactful than saying, "I'm sorry, you were declined." I never found the stockings even though she directed me where to go.

I would later discover that this was a day of taking and making wrong turns and getting lost before finding my way. The total amount for the outfit, including the earrings and necklace was a little over $127. This was, of course, without the 20% discount. I was satisfied with the cost. The outfit was a Gloria Vanderbilt outfit. I'm not always current with what happens in the news, but my daughter always keeps me informed. I would learn later that Gloria Vanderbilt, as do many designers, would rather Black people did not wear her clothing. Why, oh why, are we such hated people?

The saleslady kept apologizing that she had no larger bags in which to put the clothing. I told her that it was okay but I didn't want the hanger removed from the pants and jacket because I didn't want them to get wrinkled. She put the short bag over the top of the hanger and it covered most of the jacket. She had already folded up the blouse and it was in another bag with the jewelry. I left and found my way back to my car and out of the parking lot, exiting correctly. This would be the last "right" turn I would make.

It didn't just start to rain: it was as if buckets of water were poured out all of a sudden from the sky. I had been going 65 miles an hour and skidded a bit and had to slow down. I had a hard time seeing but managed as best I could. The rain was intermittent, as it seems to be in North Carolina most of the time, after a few moments of sunrise and clear skies. I would later discover that I got turned around because of an I-40 West detour. Somehow I was on the 26-East headed for Spartanburg. I drove about 30 miles in the wrong direction – twice. My light-hearted mood had turned. I was not happy and exasperated but determined to find my way. Twice, I had to stop at a gas station/mart to ask directions. I had some hope that I might make it to work on time. I was finally headed back on the 74-West; however, I knew that this route was a longer route, but it was a straighter shot than taking the route to the 19-South. I had passed the sign that said "Cherokee Maggie Valley." I had driven 5 miles when I saw a sign that said 20 miles to Sylva. I kept thinking I might make it to work. So, I drove 5 miles back to take the Cherokee Maggie Valley route. What a mistake! It's a shorter route in miles but it seems so much longer. By the time I passed by the casino on the US-19 it was 4:43. I was supposed to be at work in 10 minutes. There was no way. The only good thing was that it was a Monday and I knew I would only receive one point on my attendance rather than three. I had tried calling the extension for our new callout number when I was going through the mountains; however I kept getting "No Service." However, now I was able to get through. There was a recording and I left a message that I would be about an hour late. I then called the extension for the TR supervisors and Nicholas answered. I told him that I had left a message on the call out number and wanted to let them know I would be an hour late. I asked him to let Ethel know also. He said he would. My mind had gone through so many mental calisthenics earlier when I kept thinking of how I could still get to work on time. My daily ritual was being curtailed less and less. I even gave thought to maybe not showering, just throwing on my undergarments and uniform, putting on my contacts, having a bad hair day, having a bad breath day, and rushing to work. I had to catch myself. What had they done to me? I knew that I could not forego these things because I was in customer service. However, they had made me fearful of receiving points. Many good and dedicated employees have "pointed out" and were simply terminated because of this. My daughter commented that this is why the casino usually does not contest a filing for unemployment and simply pays it out. The other reason is probably because the casino can definitely afford it. Also, the casino will allow a terminated employee to come back and work for them after 90 days, 6 months, or a year, depending on the nature of the termination. However, I believed that they would not be so accommodating to someone like me. In fact, I believe they are sorry they even let me get hired in the first place. My daughter told me she was right about the employee appreciation picnic was a way for the casino to show pictures of deceptively happy slaves (I mean employees). They even went so far as to put an older Black couple on the cover with a few pictures of some of the Black people inside the EVS

Magazine. The employees on the cover were of a Black woman who was a table games supervisor and her husband. I know how PR works. This was supposed to say, "See, we don't discriminate. We love older Black people as well as younger Black people – and look – they're happy here." Never mind that there is only a handful of Black people who work there and only 1 who is a manager: a Black man named Pablo who is the Credit Manager with no staff as yet, who, by the way, never contacted me. I heard from Sara that someone from the cage will be getting the position as his assistant. The only supervisors are the table games supervisors who don't really act in full supervisory capacities. Most of the time, they serve as dealers. Luis has commented several times that he is not satisfied because he's been a dealer for over 20 years and "did not come here to deal."

I got to work and Linda counted me in with my coupons. She was asking if everything was all right; however, I just commented that everything was supposed to go smoothly because it was "my Friday." She sent me to the Rotunda after checking to make sure they had enough staff up at Earth Water. I had brought the other half of the Subway sandwich and some BBQ corn chips for lunch. Of course, I had parked on the 5th Floor in the same 5B section and relayed this to my daughter. She was working the Main Cage. She had been worried about me and had tried to call me. I told her that I started out at 1:30 pm and didn't get to work until almost 4:00pm. She couldn't believe it but was glad I was all right. I told her later to never again let me drive a distance longer than 15 miles by myself.

When I recounted the events to her, we both laughed about it when she reminded me of the episode of King of Queens with Kevin James where his character, Doug, who was an IPS (International Parcel Service) driver. Doug and his wife, Carrie, had invested Doug's $3,000 bonus check into a particular stock. They had sold the stock too early only to see it go up. They re-bought the stock and were fearful they would lose money again. While driving, the producers of the show had a monitor for the audience to see to the left which depicted the rise and fall of the stock. The hilarious part was that Doug's mood changed with the stock. When the stock was up he was jovial and speaking kindly to people who passed by. When the stock was down he was grumpy and impatient with any and everybody. This pretty much described my mood during my "lost and found" trip that day to and from Asheville. However, I would learn later that it was definitely a warning sign for me.

It was a Monday at work, but it was not as slow as it usually is. Several times we even had lines. For the most part, people trickled in periodically. Victoria commented how she and Beverly had come in from 10am to 2pm and she was back at work for the second time. She came in around 6pm. Lance was the supervisor on duty at the Rotunda. Arnette was there until about 7pm. Charles came in. Barbara came in around 7pm and Hilda came in around 9pm, I believe. Victoria said they had 24 buses that day. When I told this to my daughter, she said there couldn't have been. She worked the Main Cage and had not seen all of these people. When I dropped her off, we'd seen two buses, but who knows. I still believe Victoria was sent down there as a spy. I also know that it is no accident that Arnette works mornings while I work evenings. I believe this is the same when it comes to my daughter. I have decided to request earlier hours. I can't believe that Donald who was just hired is working better hours than me. Also, why is Ethel his supervisor? It's not fair that I have to work later hours because she didn't want to be my supervisor. I'm going to see if I can change supervisors and go on day shift. It's at least worth a try. But first, I need to know what's going to happen with the Special Events and Promotions Supervisor position.

Chapter 46

No Means No

Victoria was her old joking and jovial self. This is how I was sure she was sent to spy. I asked Arnette, before Victoria was there, if it bothered her when Poindexter comes close to her face or try to kiss her, etc. She said she was dealing with it and that it doesn't bother her like it used to. I told her that she could kindly tell him that his behavior could be considered sexual harassment. Funny, how this is the one word that I continually misspell, after having misspelled it when I was in the 7th Grade in junior high school. I got 3rd place even though I was an impromptu substitute because one of the people from our school did not show up. Thank God for the auto-correct feature in MS Word. I have got to remember: 1 R, 2 S's. Any way you spell it, what he does is sexual harassment because it's unwanted and she has told it is unwanted.

However, Arnette does not want to make waves because Poindexter is Cherokee and an enrolled member. I notice they don't say tribal member any more but enrolled member. This is probably because many of them are no longer of the tribe. There are more people of European-descent and Mexican-descent than anything else. Even with this, they only want and have been trying for years to get the Black people off their rolls. Apparently, these Black people were put on the rolls after slavery. Their former slave owners had been Indian tribal members. Again, why do they hate us so much?

I found out from Victoria that people, for some reason, think TR is the complaint department. I guess the way we're set up, where we're located when people come in, and because we are privy to a great deal of information and are expected to know "everything," makes people feel they can load us with complaints and feel somehow "justified" that they've made a bold statement. One Black woman, short hair and stature, slightly overweight, had apparently been waited on by

Charles regarding a Stay & Play offer she had received. However, based on what she told me later, Lance had told her she not eligible after talking with the front desk supervisor, the same people I talked to when trying to get a 6 or 7-digit account number to confirm their eligibility when their name was not on the Stay & Play sheet we were given. I had noticed earlier, when I went to the counter where it was posted, that it said there were none for today. I had not noticed that this was going on because I had been waiting on an attractive Black man who, I would learn later, had been with her. He and I had a good encounter and his manner seemed calm and he was grateful that I had explained to him about his reward credits, his tier score and the hidden jackpot promotion.

When she came over, she was already upset and complaining that "They lied." She said obviously we had never intended to give her the Stay & Play because her name was not on the list. She said she had called and tried to get them to book the hotel but they told her they couldn't get it on the computer and that she had to book the hotel. She said she did this and paid for it. I tried to explain things to her and let her know how it worked, mostly because I'd been through it several times now and each time learned another piece of the criteria needed to successfully get the Stay & Play. She did not want to listen, nor did she want to be consoled. I did not realize this at the time. I asked if the man I had waited on standing there was her husband. She said that "no" he was not, but that she takes care of her own business, and that nobody does that for her. I couldn't understand why she wouldn't really listen to me. I thought it was because she felt I was part of "them," or maybe she thought I was Cherokee. I told her I wanted her to have a good experience there. However, she would be comforted and left in a huff, stating that she was going to file a formal complaint. When she left, Lance thanked me that I had tried to help out.

It was not until the next day, after carefully replaying back the whole scenario to determine how I might have handled it better to make sure she was satisfied, that I realized that I could have offered her a $10 Service Recovery. All employees are authorized to give these out; however, we are not given them nor are we ever encouraged to use them. This may have worked; however, I also realized that she had a problem with me. She, like some Black women, feel intimidated by me when they hear me talk and the enemy puts enmity between me and them. Some of them are jealous of my intelligence and calm manner, especially when it comes to their Black men. She wanted to be against me and have them against me also. They want me to look bad and thereby, feel they need them to console them. I don't really take it personally because they feel it's a form of self-preservation, a way of trying to protect what they believe is theirs.

Another gentleman had come down the escalator. He had a serious look on his face and despite the fact that other reps were open, he came directly to me in the Diamond lane. I wasn't sure what he wanted but I greeted him the way I always do. He promptly told me that he had driven to Cherokee for 6-1/2 hours at the invitation of "you all" only to have "three people ignore me." He said he usually spends lots of money and visits our property at least every two weeks; however, he said he will not "spend another dime in this place." I wanted to ask him why didn't he ask to talk to someone in the Poker room, but he wasn't interested in a conversation. He simply wanted to say what he did and he promptly walked away. Victoria and the other reps talked about how they would have said something to someone in the Poker room if they had driven that long a time to get there. I was seeking to find the number to call the people in the Poker room to let them know they had lost a potential guest. Victoria said "No, don't call them." I feel as though I should have any way, but I didn't.

Hilda talked about her two dogs who she pampers and spoils and how she has them shaved ever so often. She talked about the doggy care center in Atlanta, I believe, that has French doors for the dogs' rooms and glass windows. Apparently the dogs are treated like royalty. She told us about the time she had to leave her dog for a few days and she felt so bad because it was her dog's birthday. She said that while she was away the employees at the doggy day care had given her dog a big birthday party. They gave her the pictures where the dogs had party hats and decorations, including a big cake and doggy goodies. She said how much better it made her feel to know her dog had a good time. Hilda said how she wanted to open a center just like it. Victoria told her that Ethel also wanted to open a center like that – that it was her dream. She said that Hilda should get together with Ethel and talk. I love animals; however, it amazes me how people treat them like they are their children and not just pets. In fact, they treat them better than they treat people at times.

I had worked for 5 days straight and my hands were beginning to cramp. Sunday and Monday had been heavier traffic than previously, but it was nothing compared to the previous Thursday through Saturday. It was venturing on 10pm and my back hurt and my feet. I had only one break (30 minutes) and still needed another 15-minute break. I hurt so much that I had a feeling that a 15-minute break was not going to be enough. I called for a TR supervisor on the radio. Linda answered and I requested she call me on x7181. I told her that I was in pain and needed to EO (Early Out). She told me to come on back to be counted out. When I went down to Buzz area I saw Tilly sitting in a chair and Linda was standing up reading to count me out. I said hello to Tilly and she seemed to respond. I could tell in my spirit that they had been discussing me – just what they had been discussing I wasn't sure. Linda asked me if there was anything they could do, or maybe the EMTs. I told her "no" and that I just wanted to go home. I said that my daughter would give me a massage. She mentioned her chiropractor again. I asked her to write down the number and she just gave me her doctor's name and told me to contact her in Sylva. I told her thank you. She counted me out and I had zero variance.

Chapter 47

Whose Job Is This Anyway?

August 13 – I always look for God's leading in everything. I realized that my getting lost and being turned around, including the terrible rain on Monday, was significant. My interview for the VIP Host position was scheduled for 1pm. I called Phoebe in HR around 10am and asked her if Bertha would be in the interview. She said that "yes" because Bertha was the hiring manager. I told her that I couldn't do the interview because of an Incident Report I had filed with Carlos, Manager of Employee Relations. I also left a message for Bambi and for Carlos to call me back. Phoebe called me back about 10 minutes later and said she just talked to Carlos and that I should not be afraid to attend the interview because there would be another interview person (April) and it would be a joint interview with 2 other applicants. I told her that it would still put me in a compromising situation because nothing has been resolved yet. Bambi said that they were still investigating and had not completed their report yet. I couldn't believe that they felt I would have a fighting chance to interview with and work for someone who had lied and misrepresented me.

Not long after, I got a return call from Bambi and Carlos who was also on conference. I informed her about the interview and she told me that they were aware of it. They insisted that the interview would be a group interview, but I still told them that it would put me in a compromising situation. Bambi said that the bottom line is I would still be working for Bertha. I said, "Exactly." They said they would let me know when everything was complete. I called Phoebe to ask her about the Events & Promotions Supervisor position. Now she told me that the hiring manager was going to interview someone on tomorrow (Wednesday). I asked if the person was 01, 02, or 03. I was told that I was listed as 04. Phoebe said she would find out and get back to me. I called again later and let her know that I was very, very interested in interviewing for that position.

We drove to Asheville to get lobster (Red Lobster), baby back ribs (Chili's), and hair products at Venus Beauty Supply. I did a MapQuest from where Red Lobster was located at 139 S. Tunnel Rd. However, Arnette called during that time and I wanted to make up for lost time. I couldn't get the printer to work right away and should have written the directions down but I was trying to make good time to get there and back. Arnette told me that she did not get the Service Call Attendant position. I told her I was sorry. She said that it was okay and that in the meantime she would start planning her wedding since she did have confirmation of that. I told her that "you never know" because the person could be offered the position and then change their mind, or anything could happen and she (Arnette) end up with the position anyway. She said that she would go ahead now and accept her benefits. She had originally held off because the position for which she wanted and interviewed was a part-time position.

Chapter 48

Times Change, People Don't

We made it to Asheville in good time and eventually found Venus Beauty Supply after some maneuvering. I was surprised that a whole rack of ribs at Chili's in Asheville was $19. I had paid about $6 more at the Chili's in Casa Grande, AZ. The rack had more bones than the ones in Case Grande. We found Venus Beauty Supply in West Asheville. While I was waiting in the car for Sara, I watched a couple who appeared to be neighbors rather than close friends, at least this was the impression I got from the bits and pieces of their conversation. One lady was a White woman and the other was a Black woman. It was an older car and they were putting all of the groceries in the car as they talked and kept looking at me looking at them. The White woman was driving so I decided she was giving the Black woman a ride to the store to help her.

I started thinking about the Black people who lived in North Carolina. I don't believe many of them intentionally moved to North Carolina. It's my guess that they have been here since their ancestors who were in slavery in North Carolina, Tennessee, South Carolina, Georgia, Virginia, Florida, Mississippi, and Alabama. I can see the same slavery mindset on many of them. They seem complacent just to be past Jim Crow laws. Our ancestors were freed in 1896, that is, the law was passed. Lincoln asked what the slaves wanted and they said they each wanted 40 acres and a mule. They wanted sovereignty just like what the Natives enjoy right now. They wanted to make their own laws and govern themselves. However, a conspiracy allowed John Wilkes Booth to shoot and kill President Lincoln. President Johnson took office and reversed the order. He gave everything back to our former slave owners and we had virtually no rights. Our ancestors were still treated like slaves but in a different way, just like today. They were still lynched, raped, and unjustly thrown in prison to work long and hard hours. They were at least content that they were no longer legally considered slaves. "Freedom" would not come until 1935; however, Jim Crow laws prevented them from enjoying their "freedom" until the 1960's during the Civil Rights Movement. Again, many were murdered and discriminated against. So, our ancestors marched non-violently. They cried out for their basic rights. They shouted "we shall overcome" and they tried to overcome their lower class status by reaching deep within themselves. and shouted "I'm Black and I'm proud!" They fought for Title VII of the Civil Rights Act, only to have the Natives discount this by enjoying sovereignty and the Indian Preference Act of 1934 with more rights extended to 1974 whereby they have legal protection from the federal government to legally discriminate against us. A great number of these Natives were our ancestors' former slave owners as well.

I researched and researched and asked questions until I talked with someone at the legislative branch of the federal government. I wanted to know just how far the Indian Preference Act extended. Could they also apply this to job status change from full-time to part-time? Could they apply it to preference with regard to time schedules and paid time off? Could they post jobs that were listed solely for Natives or enrolled members? The gentleman on the other line, whose voice I could recognize as a Black man, said "Yes, they can." I was appalled. I told him that we (Black people) needed a reservation so we could receive per capita and protection from the federal government. He sort of laughed, but I was completely serious.

I know a great deal of black people don't realize that this is the case. There are a lot of enrolled members who are of European and Mexican descent. Only a few are of African descent and they (Natives) are trying their best to rid themselves of the Blacks whose ancestors were on the rolls because they had been former slaves. From working at Gila River Indian Community, I do know that they wanted to rid themselves of a great number of Mexican Americans because they felt they were the ones who brought the drugs and the gangs into their neighborhoods. However, this situation does not seem to be prevalent in Cherokee as it was in Sacaton, AZ.

August 14 – Today, I got a call from Carlos' secretary. She said she was calling on his behalf and wanted me to come in this Friday at 4pm for a meeting. I told her I would be there. My mind is imaging what they have decided. I leave it in God's hands. I wanted confirmation of whether or not the Special Events & Promotions Supervisor position is mind. I asked God that if it is his will that they would remove the write-ups from my file. If not, then the write-ups would stay. I leave all things in his powerful and wise hands.

Jack called and asked me how I was doing today. I told him I was fine. He said he was trying to "squeeze more hours out of everyone" and wanted to know if I could come in for a 10-hour shift on tomorrow (Thursday) and work from 12pm to 10pm. I told him I'd be there at 12.

Chapter 49

Safer Gambling

It's been a relaxing day. Caesar's Entertainment stock closed at 18.25 today. It had gone down a few points from yesterday. However, it still has been going up. Not sure what will happen later. I know that I need to put money into my brokerage account so I can invest in what Stansberry Financial has recommended. I don't have much to invest but I realize this is something that our people have not been taught to do. Most are too busy trying to take care of their families, put food on their table, and keep a roof over their heads. We've been fighting so many battles for simple and basic rights that investing in our future has not been a normal practice. Comparatively, only a few enjoy this practice. I've learned that this is the best and safest type of "gambling" in which anyone should participate. The slots, tables, and poker should be considered a leisure activity with minimum "investment," all the while understanding that this money could be gone forever. It is true that the crash of 1929 sent many people crashing themselves to the ground in response to losing their money. The fallout of 1986 caused much grief and Obama later felt he needed to bail out the banks because they were "too big to fail."

There are many professional poker players who make a good living. My daughter has a goal to do this. It is something about No Limit and being "All In" that scares the heck out of me, even when I'm playing "free" poker tournaments such as in the Atlanta Poker Club (APC) or Interstate Poker League. You can buy lunch and/or dinner and receive additional chips for your purchase. Some of the restaurants and/or bars & grills offer the winners bar cash. Sometimes they put up actual cash for monthly tournaments for the players with the highest scores for the month, for the quarter, and for the year. Some of the players invest a great deal of money because they play 2 to 3 times a day for 7 days a week.

Let's say they spend an average $20 for each tournament played. For the APC league a player starts off with 1500 chips and can only spend up to a maximum of $25 to get an extra 3,000 chips at some venues and an extra 4000 chips at other venues. Sometimes there is an extra 1000 chips for special days such as federally-recognized holidays and Halloween, St. Patrick's Day, Mother's Day and Father's Day. However, the players have to either wear the designated colors or a button or APC apparel. The Interstate league is the older of the two leagues. While APC is touted as the most professional and prides itself in this fact, the truth is there are pros and cons of both leagues. APC league has more White players than other races while Interstate has more Black players and other races. APC uses tables that have been covered with cloth. Even though they are different colors, some of them are tattered, stained, and worn. Interstate uses World Series of Poker professional tables. APC's chips are plain and cheap and have no dollar amounts on them. Usually the white chips are $25, black chips are $100, the yellow chips are $500, the red chips are $1000 and the orange chips are $2000. Dealers who are also players can get an extra $1000 for dealing initially and another $1000 after the break which usually comes after the first hour of the tournament. If the dealers are certified they receive an extra $1500 for dealing initially and another $1500 after the break, that is, if they are still dealing and haven't gone out of the tournament. Players can become VIP card holders by paying $99 for six months and $199 for a year. VIP players receive an extra $1000 in chips for each tournament they play, no matter how many tournaments they play per day.

In the Interstate league a player starts off with 1200 chips. They can get $500 extra for wearing Interstate apparel and dealers can get an extra $1000 total for dealing. The leagues are set up such that the restaurants and bars/grills can be listed as a green, yellow, or red venue. If they are a green venue a player can buy chips 3 times during the tournament; if they are a yellow venue, a player can buy chips 4 times during the tournament; if they are a red venue, there is absolutely no limit to how many times a player can "chip up" as they call it. Dealers in the Interstate league receive a total of $1000 chips during the whole time they deal. Of course, some tournament directors are more lax on this and I have received a total of $2000 chips if still dealing after the break. Interstate chips are labeled with chip amounts. Dealers are never certified in the Interstate league and almost anyone who wants to deal can deal if they ask the tournament director beforehand.

I have played in both leagues and even became a certified dealer in the APC league. To become certified, a player has to deal at least 40 hours within a quarter. They then have to take the online course, attend at least one live hands-on training, pass the written test, and pass a live evaluation. I had started dealing during the APC pre-games. During these games, players can win extra $500 chips for either winning with designated hands such as 7-2 any suit or red 7's, etc. They can earn them by setting up or taking down tables for the tournament director or losing with pocket Kings or Aces. These all depend on what each tournament director has designated and had approved by the APC Director. It was a lot of fun; however, like everything else there were problems, clicks, and, of course, racial discrimination. I got to deal more in the Interstate league than APC – either way I got a lot of practice.

When my daughter and I first started playing in the APC league we seemed to be welcomed. We started playing on Friday mornings way in Lilburn, GA at Mama Mia's Restaurant because Sara worked at Lanier Technical College in Gwinnett, GA. So, Friday at 12 noon was the only day we were initially able to play. It was a 35-mile drive there. Sometimes we wondered why we were driving that distance and buying chips. Most of the time we got out within the first 30 minutes due to bad beats. As time went on, we both started to win some of the tournaments. However, Sara was no longer working. She was attending school online during the times she came to Georgia. I was only making minimal money from the business, but mostly we did not buy extra chips. There were a few times that we won the tournaments by starting with only the $1500 chips. I kept telling them that the game was 90% luck and maybe 10% skill – usually the bluffing factor involved. However, they disagreed with me. We played at the Arizona Pub on Monday evening until it was no longer an APC venue, Bench Warmers on Monday evening thereafter, Loco's on Tuesday and Thursday evening, Famous Pub a few times and Sledge Lounge thereafter on Wednesday evenings, Mama Mia's on Friday afternoons, Zuffy's sometimes on Friday evenings, Zuffy's on Saturday afternoons, and Tin Roof Cantina on Sunday afternoons. I discovered that they were right: the game was not luck; it was a pure waste of my time.

Chapter 50

A Date When Employees Related

August 15 – Today I had to work a 10-hour shift, from 12pm to 10pm. It was a bit difficult. I took my first 2 15-minute breaks then my 30-minute break and another 15-minute. It was pretty busy. Edward said they expected to hit $25 million. We were told in Buzz to makes sure we try to take our breaks as close to the correct times as possible and come back when we're supposed to do so. We were also told that we can no longer put door stops in the doors or paper in the door to the Buzz area when we clock in at the other time clock. Apparently, surveillance is tracking this. I know that this has been heightened because of my Incident Report.

I went down to the Rotunda. Several reps with the same first names were there; one is a D/R. The other two are short; one reminds me of the wife on the TV show King of the Hill. Arnette was there for a brief moment. She looked concerned and told me so. We discussed briefly about the situation with Poindexter. I had told her the previous day to never be alone with him for her own protection. She said she was led to have the police dispatch phone number ready with her at all times. She had told me that Poindexter had said a couple of months back that if she told anybody on him he would cut off her head and throw her body in the lake. She said he was deep into the occult and is supposed to be a "medicine man." I've warned her that if he keeps bothering her that she needs to report it.

Lance was the D/R on duty after Fran left. It was pretty busy and steady but not so much so to have several people doing a 10-hour shift. Beverly was complaining about it. It seems we're getting a lot of confusing information about the Stay & Play. Beverly said the people in the Service Center are giving people the wrong information.

I notice that both Beverly and Zelda have earlier hours than I do. Why is this? Both of them were hired after me. It's interesting how they never had to fight for full-time or anything else, but I, unfortunately, seem to have to fight for everything I get.

Brad told me about the date he had previously. Apparently he met her at a Harley-Davidson bike shop. He said he'd been planning to get another one. He's an associate pastor, a heavy-set man with a personality that is like a congenial motorcycle gang member. He said they both like to rescue horses. From what he said she is a "nice Christian girl." I told him that they say "the third time's a charm." He said, "Yes, they do say that, don't they." His voice sounded a bit whimsical with a glimmer of hope. I was half-kidding Brad when I said, "Brad had a hot date the other day." He smiled, "Rachel you are a gossip." I told him that "Oh, sure I'm gossiping when I say that in front of you, but Linda wasn't gossiping when she talked about you having been married twice." He said he was just kidding. I told him that I would never say it behind his back, and that this would be gossiping if I did that.

Ethel counted me out with zero-variance.

August 16 – I dropped off my daughter on the lower level around 11am. I am tired because of her morning hours and my swing shift hours. I know it's taking a toll on her also. I had the meeting with Carlos at 4pm but my shift didn't start until 6pm. I knew it was going to be another long day. I had to get dressed for my shift because I was not sure how long the meeting would last. I parked on the 5th floor and took the staff elevator down to the 1st floor. You have to swipe your badge when you're going to the first floor. I'm told this is so that non-employees do not have access. It concerns me a bit because I've worked at places where I know they can be really dirty. They can de-activate your badge without you being aware of it and then you're caught inside the elevator.

When I didn't know about swiping my badge the first time I accessed the staff elevator, I couldn't understand why it wasn't going anywhere and there was no emergency button. I felt claustrophobic and thought for a moment that I would suffocate inside and be found dead in the elevator. Even though we're told we have to park on the 5th Floor, I think I'll let Sara know that it may be a good idea to take the stairs or just park in the lower lot every day and take the shuttle, or just pay $5 each day to park across the street. God will lead and guide me as to what to do and when. I know he has my back in every situation. All I have to do is follow his leading and his timing.

I put my things in my locker and went up to the 2nd Floor where I was told to meet Carlos. I found his office but he was not there. I was early – it was only 3:50pm. I noticed that Pearl was the only Employee Relations person who was in. I told her who I was and that I didn't know where I was supposed to wait. She came out and told me that we had a couple of options. She led me to the Mother's Room with 2 old-fashioned chairs with long round cushions for the back. I noticed a few Parenting magazines on the wooden table. I flipped through one of them while I waited. After a few minutes, I put the magazine down, just folded my hands, and closed my eyes. I saw a man appear in the door with folders in his hands. I assumed he was Carlos and I got up to shake hands. He introduced himself and said we were going to go up to Bambi's office. Carlos looked more Mexican than Native. When I looked at all of the pictures of the Cherokee Leaders posted on the first floor hallway, there was only one who looks more Cherokee. None of them are "red-skinned." They look more European than anything else and some look more Mexican than anything else. Of course, Natives and Mexicans are all of the Mongoloid family.

I told Carlos that I didn't start my shift until 6pm, that's why I wore my uniform. He said that sometimes departments will allow you to start your shift early. I would learn later that Ethel would not allow me to do this. Carlos presented me with copies of pages on the Hiring Process and Indian Preference that seemed to be from the Employee Manual. This is information I already had. He then began to explain the same things Bambi and others had said to me. What they didn't seem to get is that I needed to make sure they were following the procedures and were being fair and just with the policies when it came to me; it wasn't that I didn't know what was supposed to be done. I just had to learn (the hard way) the little details of specific procedures such as applying internally versus apply externally.

He also gave me a copy of the July 1-31 Efficiency Report that had the number of transactions. He said this was not the matrix. He also gave me a copy of the matrix that they supposedly used to determine who would be offered a full-time position. He explained about "department need" being a justification. The matrix had various criteria that Ivan had mentioned; however, he told me that they took all of the employees' names off of the sheet, including mine. Why can't I see what I scored? I also told Carlos that I had told Ivan that I did not disagree with the matrix and the criteria he used, but I disagreed with the fact that they were measuring employees who had only been there for 3 weeks against employees who had been there 90 days. I told him that Ivan had said I didn't trust his judgment. I told him that this wasn't the case, but that my disagreement did not entail non-compliance. I just felt it was unfair to me. I relayed to Carlos my communication with Penny in HR regarding the matrix and the posting of the TR rep position. I realize that he already had talked to them.

I tried to be as congenial as possible and said it was a shame that I had to go to this length to get a copy of the matrix because I had asked for it several times. He said that Ivan probably didn't give me a copy because other employees might use it and start filling it in to measure themselves and their co-workers. If everything is fair and equal, why can't they do this? The most interesting thing in the whole meeting is that Carlos said that even before I brought this whole incident up and received the write-ups, they had already heard about the call with Olga in HR. He looked to Bambi who confirmed it. He said that Olga put the phone up in the air and he could hear me on the other line. This was to imply that I had been shouting. I did not ask him what he heard me saying because I knew this was all a contrived lie. They were trying to find something after the fact to cover up both Olga and Bertha's misdeeds. I told him that if he heard me then the volume on the phone must have been amplified because I don't have a loud voice. I told him that I don't yell at people, that it's not something I do. I told him they could talk to my co-workers who would tell them the same thing. They both know from talking to me that I have a soft-spoken voice. I kept my composure the whole time. I told him that I was not trying to discount what he was saying, but gave my logical version of it. I looked over at Bambi and realized that she was not on my side either. Carlos said that at that point they didn't see anything whereby they could remove it from my file. He said that it could have been worded differently.

The point is the whole thing was a pack of lies. What were they going to do with the words "unprofessional," "rude," and "aggressive"? These are extremely damaging and they know it. That's why it was done in the first place. I realize that all of them had been setting a precedence to make me out to be something that I'm not. As the Bible say, they hate me without a cause. Carlos stated that if he were looking at a prospective candidate's file he would be more concerned with the lack of following procedures, etc. This is ridiculous! These write-ups were for 1) not stamping a receipt "VOID"; 2) Having a $10 variance in coupons; 3) writing a coupon for Host Cash for a 7-Star guest (he was delighted); 4) writing a replacement coupon that had expired the previous day; 5) writing a replacement coupon for a Diamond player that had already been re-written by another rep but had not been redeemed at the time I wrote it (this one I signed in protest). I was told at the time that everybody gets these; however, they seemed to carry more weight as being detrimental to me than anybody else. I told Carlos that the 2 write-ups I had received for which I was protesting were the most damaging. I told him that I had applied for the Special Events & Promotions Supervisor position (no one said a word), and that if I were a manager and saw that in someone's file, that is not a person I would consider for the position. There was a brief silence because this is exactly what they were trying to do to me. Carlos also told me to contact his office instead of HR in the future with the kinds of questions I had. He said that sometimes when their office gets involved, the managers will respond quicker. I told him about leaving a message for Delilah with regard to why I was not hired for the Sr. Acct. Executive Casino Host position for which I interviewed on July 4th and had not heard from her. He said he was not excusing her but that they had a lot of things going on in their department and then she went on vacation. Yes, he was trying to excuse her.

So, basically they were going to do nothing just as Sara had said. She told me later that we needed it in writing, that is, we needed to get their report. I told her they were probably not going to give me this. She said we needed to get this writing. I know it must have been the Lord who had my disposition the way it was before going into the meeting. I kept imagining the worst – that they would fire me for no reason, or set me up some way so it looks like they have a reason. I realize how vulnerable I am by working there. They can pretty much do anything they want, but Oh, that is, if it were not for God! It's very difficult because I know I'm going to have to file with EEOC and try to get a right to sue letter. I really hate all of this stuff. I'm the person who only wants there to be love and harmony but the enemy will not allow it. God is a mighty force and he will fight my battles. The enemy seems to be getting the upper hand, but my God is all powerful, righteous, and his glory is from everlasting to everlasting.

Chapter 51

Are Your Numbers Up?

During Buzz Ethel talked about brainstorming ideas as to how they can get their Friendly /Helpful scores back up. She stressed how the below 67% score has been "unheard of" since she's been there during her 3 years+. I realize at this point that the devil is using her to "pick" at me like she was doing Arnette. I remember saying that the surveys they take are so subjective and that there are a lot more factors involved. Guests could have just lost their money. Usually, they only remember the very last experience they have. You can do 99 things right out of a 100, but it is the 1 time that is not quite right that people remember. It doesn't have to be something you did wrong. This is a gambling and entertainment industry. The whole goal is to show you a good time while you are slowly being bled out of your money. You are left pale as a ghost and drained but the good news you're dying with a smile on your face. This is because ignorance is bliss.

Today was the day 7-Star players were previewing the items for the Shopping Spree from 10am to 6pm. Sara told me later that there were so many people and that the line was all the way from the 2nd Floor Promotions area back to Brio's Italian Tuscan Grill restaurant. She was working up there and she said everything they put on does not work well.

I always ask Diamond players about their Diamond Celebration $100 Dinner coupon because I don't want them to miss out. I'm really surprised how many of them are unaware that it exists. In fact, I'm always surprised that a great number of players are unaware of what their RC's are, how they can be used and/or redeemed, and what their tier score is. Most don't know what the different levels of players' cards are. They don't know that they have to play once every six months at one of our over 40 properties to keep their reward credits. It appears that Harrah's Cherokee Casino & Resort is run much differently from the other Caesar's Entertainment properties. I'm finally understanding that the Eastern Bank of Cherokee Nation bought a franchise from Caesar's. The Cherokees signed an agreement that they would control their Human Resources department. However, it gets a bit complicated because everything says Equal Employment Opportunity but this is a misnomer.

I've had guests who have told me, "You're so sweet," "You're going a great job," and "Thank you, you've been so helpful." I even had one lady say that she's going to send a letter to Mendleson because she likes to acknowledge people who are especially helpful. When I showed her my badge, she sort of looked down. She was of European-descent. It seems as though some people try to get you to want something but when it appears you want it, they wield what they think is power and control, and then they work to make sure you don't get it. This is the enemy at work. Oh, but God Almighty!

I noticed that I've seen men of European-descent, all younger than me, who wear badges that say Senior Account Executive Casino Host. I've only seen one African-descent male who had this same title. He was a bald, effeminate man with glasses named Peter. Victoria and Felicia seemed to flock around him like bees to honey. I knew the enemy was having them do that as if to show they were not discriminatory and because they all knew I interviewed for that position. It's always the enemy's plan to make you feel less than and cause division at the same time. They wanted to make sure I don't have a chance to tell him how I've been treated. Oh, but God will find a way.

I remember on this day that I was extremely tired and my whole body ached. I have got to slow down because it's wearing me out. I remember sitting between Victoria and Brad. Brad announced that it was someone's birthday. I believe there were 4 of us and they sang Happy Birthday to the guest. I didn't join in because my arms ached and I was helping another guest. Little did I know I would hear about this in Buzz the next day. However, I went home with my back, shoulder, feet, arms, and fingers aching.

Felicia counted me out and I had zero variance. As I was leaving from the Motor Coach area to go out to the first floor parking where the buses come through, I noticed Ethel coming in from outside. I thought this was odd because she's usually not there until 2:30 am. I saw Sara sitting outside waiting for me. Little did I know that the next day there would be a change in policy written in the Daily News, the internal communication from HR.

Chapter 52

Happy, Happy Birthday

August 17 – During Buzz, Ethel had already told us about the promotions going on. She said the Shopping Spree would be going on from 10am to 8pm. I was working from 4pm to 12:30am. Then something interesting happened. I started to leave to go to the Rotunda and she told me to wait a minute. She went over again what she had already said about the promotions going on and added: "Rachel, please make sure we all join in the birthday song because the guests really like it." I was stunned. I said "Well. . . okay." However, I hesitated and added, "Okay, but I'm going to have to get that one in writing." I left out. I knew it was the enemy at work. She is just another one of his imps. I knew that she was going to put something in my file later. I was outdone because she said that in front of Barbara. Barbara is aware that if anybody, I always sing. One time it was only Barbara and I and I had her sing, twice – once for my guest and then for her guest. I knew that it had to be no one except Victoria who had said this to Ethel. I realize that she is not to be trusted. She is another one of the enemy's imps. They hate me without a cause. Also, Victoria has so much control there. Because she's been there for over 6 years and does the training, they treat her like she's one of the supervisors. However, this should not be. She likes the responsibility and control without the accountability. If anyone is unprofessional, it is these people. However, God is always on his throne.

When we were being counted out for the night by Ethel, they were talking about the birthday song. I quickly brought up about the little lady who had announced when I was waiting on her, "I'm 60 years old today!" I had said to Brad, "We have a birthday today." We all sang to her and even the guests who were in line and standing at the counters all joined in.

Felicia had asked if I was doing okay and I said I was fine. I didn't offer anything else because I'm sure she would find out about the outcome or lack thereof from Employee Relations.

On shift at the Rotunda there was Donald, Brad, Sean (after 12am when Earth Water closed), Hilda at 8pm, Victoria, and Barbara. Donald went home at 9pm and Brad went home at 10pm. I found out that Victoria had been instrumental in getting early hours for Donald. I know that they don't want me to have early hours because the devil wants to keep Arnette and I apart. There is absolutely no reason why Victoria was assigned to Felicia as her supervisor when Ethel had been her supervisor all along. I know she is there as a spy to see what I am doing and saying. I no longer share anything with her. Felicia is nice and sweet to me; however, I know that she gossips – something a supervisor should not do. Victoria was in her office with Muriel when I was leaving to go get counted out. She's just too comfortable. However, God is answering my prayer. I asked him to reveal everything that is done is secret and shout on the rooftops all that is spoken in secret by the enemy.

They had the free concert – two White women who were singing Bluegrass songs. I usually like different types of music but it did not have any variation to it. Most of us thought it was completely awful. Barbara said that it was just too loud. Donald and Hilda kept making comments about how awful it was and said they were wondering when it was going to end. I relayed Donald's comments when I went to the Buzz area to be counted out. I notice Linda was in there also. I believe it was Lauren Alaina. I told Hilda that I know why the concert was free. Victoria had been making "how-down" gestures, as if she was playing a washboard. I told Felicia that I could play the jug. We were laughing and having a good time, but I'm still not fooled by the enemy. They can smile all the while stabbing you in the back and laugh while they twist the knife even deeper. My God shall supply all my needs and fight all my battles.

Brad told me that we can no longer drop off and pick up anyone on the lower level of the parking lot where the buses come in and out. Felicia said it was only for supervisors and above. Again, it was the enemy's way of reminding me that I did not even get interviewed for the supervisor position in Promotions. I felt a bit let down because it seems they were determined to make like harder for us. Sara was not happy when I told her. She said they keep making people think they care about their employees, but this is simply not true. I told Sara we would just have to leave a bit earlier, that's all. I told her we'd have to just drop off and pick up on the 3rd floor or in front of the hotel area. Either way, we'd do what we have to do. The fact that this comes from HR communications tells me that they are reacting to my incident report and the devil is trying to make life harder. Praise be to God for his goodness! The devil is a liar.

Sara surprised me and cooked macaroni and cheese, corn, and Tilapia. I was a happy camper. I watched a little of Everybody Loves Raymond and some King of Queens. I only remember a re-run episode of Everybody Loves Raymond where Deborah accidently threw out a letter Ray had received from Muhammad Ali. I went to bed right after eating and talking briefly with Sara. She had spent $80 at Food Lion. She just doesn't realize how much I appreciate her. I pray that God blesses her 100 times over for the good daughter that she's been to me.

I talked to Reese earlier that day and we agreed about the reparations, the join lawsuits, and what we need to do. He gave me the number of the attorney that his attorney recommended for his civil case. Before I contact her, I told Reese I want to set up a website because I need to get more people involved. I did some research and found that the Rastafarians in Kingston, Jamaica had a rally at the West

Indies University where they had petitioned Queen Elizabeth II in Britain to get reparations for slavery. This opened up my mind a bit more. I realize that there are a lot of little fires that have been started and are going on; however, nothing will be accomplished until we combine them into a huge blaze. I know there may be obstacles because the homosexuals will want to join in our fight because they think their struggle is about civil rights when their fight is not the same as ours. It is just a trick of the enemy. Other races are going to complain because they don't understand that "injustice anywhere is a threat to justice everywhere." Ignorant Black people with slave mentality are going to complain because they are afraid of what might happen. They don't want the applecart upset because their false image of apples might be exposed. They know they have no apples in their carts, but no one bothers them, so they are content. However, the time is now to stand up and be counted. Evil prospers when good men (and women) do nothing. I have to take what they're doing to me but God has his own timing and I won't react to the devil's promptings. Oh, Father, let your expert and loving hand lead and guide me from day to day.

I had zero variance for the day.

August 18 – Today is Sunday and the guest traffic is of course slower than Saturday; however, it seems pretty steady down at the Rotunda. Ethel seems to be gone because Linda counted us in and did the Buzz. I look on the sheet and notice that it's Linda's birthday. So, I silently sing the TR Birthday Song to her. She laughs lightly and thanks me. When she mentions this, Leslie says we should sing Happy Birthday to Linda. She and Victoria sing the traditional song and I comment how that version is boring. I sang a few bars of the more upbeat soulful version.

Linda is trying to elicit ideas to help improve our Friendly/Helpful customer service skills. They brainstorm and come with a few more such as: go above and beyond the expectations of your guest and to ask when you don't the answers instead of making up something as you go along. It never dawned on me that some of the staff did not implement this. I commented that if you have to tell them that, then it makes you wonder how they even got the job in the first place. I said that it was just basic customer service. I was in sort of an intolerant mood that day, mostly because I was tired. Sara's morning schedule and my swing shift do not jive because we only have the one car. Both of us are losing sleep. No matter what time I go to bed, I still wake up around 5am. I think about things and finally get up about an hour or two later and write.

Linda asked where we wanted to go. Leslie said she wanted to go upstairs and Victoria said she wanted to go to the Rotunda. I said I wanted to go home. Linda laughed and said that I couldn't go there. I told her I'd go to the Rotunda. Donald and Brad were there. So were Arnette and Poindexter. Poindexter kept giving me mean, direct looks. I just laughed it off. I don't know if he thought he was going to intimidate me or try to put a curse on me, like Arnette talked about, but I let him know without words that he has no power over me. I notice that he seemed aloof when it came to me yet he was down at the other end talking with Arnette on one side and I don't remember who the other female was. Victoria and Jeffrey commented a few minutes after Poindexter left about how Poindexter was more "hyper" than usual. I told Arnette that I believed he uses drugs but no one does anything about it or says anything about it. I know this is because he's a tribal member. Even if you consider this use of whatever type of drug it is a tribal custom, it has no place in the workplace.

I remember when I worked for Maricopa County Public Schools and I was assigned to one of the mountain schools. It was over an hour's drive to work. The school was a K-12 school for the Native community. I was a long-term substitute and taught Math to the 3rd Graders. I remember one student,

Jose, who pushed his Math book onto the floor. I let it stay there and went to help the other students. I watched him out of the corner of my eye and he eventually picked up his book. He seemed so strange but I didn't really know how to reach him. The next day he hung himself. They said he'd always wanted a CD player; however, it was his brother who received one for his birthday. Jose apparently was trying to get attention and had tied sheets around his neck. However, they found scratches around his neck where it looked like he tried to free himself, but to no avail. I remember that I couldn't go to the funeral because someone had to teach the classes which they combined that day. However, I did go over at lunch time to where the funeral was being held and took a card of condolences. I noticed several males who were in prison clothes wearing shackles on their wrists and ankles. I realized that a number of those kids had no real positive role models because many of the males were incarcerated.

Because of the tragedy, a wealthy husband and wife, who remained anonymous, donated a truckload of CD players to the school for the children. It was a great gesture; however, it was like putting a bandage over cancer. No one ever really got to the root of the problem. There were 9-year-olds who I was surprised to find out actually smoked weed. On the playground I casually talked with one of my students. I tried to hide my dismay when she said nonchalantly, "Oh, smoking cigarettes is not good for you, but smoking week is good." Her family performed ceremonial rituals where passing the "peace pipe" was a common thing. I was a bit naïve when it came to the culture, but I learned pretty quickly.

Chapter 53

Jackpots and Crackpots

I talked briefly with Arnette about Poindexter's sexual harassment. I could see the pain on her face. She told me she had the number of police emergency just in case.

People were still coming in for the Shopping Spree. We noticed the confusion because Promotions does not provide enough detailed information in their marketing materials. If you combine this with the fact that guests don't always read the information that they are given and the fact that our Service Call Center is not well informed and gives out the wrong information, you have a pretty well-organized mess on your hands. In addition, guests thought they did not have to register for the spree if they only wanted to redeem half of their promotional credits for free slot play. From what I gathered from one of the guests who spoke to someone in Promotions, they had to register in advance anyway. Several guests were disillusioned and disappointed. I truly wish they would give me a shot at the supervisor position in the Promotions Dept. I know I could make a difference; however, prejudice and racism has, once again, prevented me from being the asset and help improve things. I still know that if God wants me to have the position, I'll have it in spite of everything else and everyone else.

The Hidden Jackpot promotion is still going strong. One of the things I've noticed, and I believe Ethel commented on it also, was that Promotions will post details in Keyweb (via the Promotions link) about an event such as the Hidden Jackpot Millionaire-Maker. However, the details may get revised later but we're still operating on the old information. They need to post something in red that says "New" or "Revised" to flag it, or email to a supervisor and/or manager in a time fashion. I believe they try but somehow the ball gets dropped. Sometimes the frontline staff just does not read the important communication and just go by the bits and pieces that they hear. I was prone to this until I started reading the promotion information. Of course, there is always human error. I noticed that the Overview of the Hidden Jackpot promotion said that the guests could win up to $5000 in free slot play. This was a typo because the most the guests could win was $500.

This is why things need to be proofread backwards and forwards. Sometimes people think one little digit or punctuation mark does make a difference. However, historical events have proven just how catastrophic these "little" mistakes can be. It's not always the big things that get us; it's the little foxes that can be devastating. Here are some examples. I make a binding deal by my signature where I wanted to pay $500 for an old used car; however, I didn't notice that the seller of the car had either on purpose or mistakenly added an extra zero on the sales price in the contract. This is why you should always read very carefully anything before you sign it. Another more devastating example would be a doctor prescribing 500 mg of a drug to a patient. However, anyone who has ever tried to read a doctor's prescription knows they usually have terrible handwriting. If, for whatever reason, the nurse or the pharmacist translated this prescription by either thinking the "m" was another "0" or missing the "m" entirely and giving the patient 500 g (grams) instead, not only would the patient suffer tremendously, but in many cases would result in the patient's death.

Here's one of more historical note; however, the result was a life-saving one rather than tragic. Czarina Maria Fyodorovna saved a man's life by misplacing a comma in an edit that was written by her husband Alexander III. The edit was supposed to read "Pardon impossible, to be sent to Siberia." The man was set free after the Czarina changed the comma to read "Pardon, impossible to be sent to Siberia." His life was saved, simply due to a misplaced mark of punctuation.

Hilda is always full of stories to tell. She had Barbara, Victoria, and me laughing. She talked about a guy who was an arrogant police officer. Apparently he was married but wanted to date Hilda. She said he would say things like, "I can't believe you let me leave." Hilda said he had huge bulging muscles, blonde hair and blue eyes. She says "He was gorgeous" in that thick Tennessee accent of hers.

Lance was the D/R. Muriel came in at 11pm as usual. She had baked brownies for Linda's birthday. She put icing on top and walnuts inside. They were very good. When I was leaving they told me to take one. I said playfully, "Oh, take two they're small" and waited for someone to object. No one did. I just took one of them and told Muriel, "My lips say take two, but my hips say take one." She laughed. I know that the supervisors have access to our Personnel files in the Dept., so I wonder if the D/R know about what's going on with Employee Relations. I know they see the emails. It takes a lot getting used to, that is, not being in the loop with emails. Even when I worked at Gila River Indian Community, I had my own employee email account. However, I realize I'm working in a totally different employment community – one like I've never experienced. I know that the tribe still has a long way to go.

Linda counted me out. I had zero- variance.

Chapter 54

Disharmony is a Familiar Song

August 19 – Sara and I had a disagreement because she said her manager gave her the go-ahead to still pick up and drop off at the lower level parking lot. I was tired and sleepy but couldn't get her to understand that it didn't matter that she was driving I would still be seen as dropping her off. Of course the buses were there and one of the TR employees was checking them in. It was around 11am. My daughter can be stubborn at times. She made a comment about Ethel being the devil and me going by what she says. Even though it's quite possible Ethel had a hand in getting this policy changed, in all fairness it was communicated in the Daily News. This was what I meant when I told Ethel the other day that I'd have to see it in writing with regard to us having to sing the birthday song. However, I notice that she had handwritten on the slate on the left wall in the Buzz area that every staff member should be participating in the TR birthday song. This is why I waited until Victoria left to privately say to Linda (even though Nicholas, Leslie and Eunice were in there) that I'm usually the one who sings the birthday song. I even had Barbara sing it twice because her guest and my guest both had birthdays that day. I told Linda, who already knew, that I was in pain that day which was the only time I didn't participate in the birthday song. I told her how Victoria had told Ethel and Ethel singled me out and said what she said to me. Linda didn't think that was right. I told her that it seems everybody takes full notice when you do something wrong or seemingly do something wrong, but nobody says anything when you do something right. Linda told me that it was going to change.

Linda told us about her sister who is a marketing executive for Mary Kay and how they were able to take charge of their department by tracking and isolating what customer service problems were due to their department versus those problems due to other departments. Linda said she was going to make up a little sheet whereby we could check off the different problems as they arise. This way we could keep a tally. I told her how I had made, but didn't use, a little sheet I wanted my guest to fill out. I think what she's going to do is great. It's about time. I know that some of those in charge are not truly qualified, but Linda is. I know that since I have been there these past 5 months, there is not one time that Ethel has ever given me any "kudos" for anything I've done. This was even before I reported to Felicia. I only see Felicia 3 days out of the week about 2 hours each time. She checks with me to make sure things are all right, but that's it. I still never had the "Get Me" or "Root for Me." However, my write-ups and dings in my Personnel File serve as the "Guide Me."

I really wish they had allowed me to get the position as the Cherokee Leader Associate. I know that I could have helped in so many ways. However, they don't want to give this Black woman that much power and/or authority. In most cases, they don't really want things to change, but if changes have to be made, they are all right with either an enrolled member or a person of another race doing so.

Brad, Victoria, Nicole, Alexis, Louise, and Arnette were at the Rotunda. Arnette was commenting that she really had to pray. She said she was like a "cat in heat." She said that she could feel it all over her when Poindexter touched her. I told her that those were sex spirits he was trying to impose upon her. She couldn't understand why it was hitting her so hard. I told her that the enemy will keep picking and picking at you until he finally breaks down your barrier, if he can. I told her that she needed to go on the Internet and look up "Succubus" but I didn't tell her about "Incubus." These were male and female sex demons. One of them was the male sex demon and the other was the female sex demon. They enemy uses both of them on either males or females. This is also where the homosexual drive comes from. People don't realize that this is what is happening. It is a daily struggle to get past these spirits. Since she talked about how Poindexter would use words to her as his "sex slave," I told her she needs to use the Word of God against him. If he is so bold as to speak those words to her, she needs to be even bolder in the Spirit of Christ and speak God's holy word to him. I reminded her of how Jesus, who had fasted for 40 days and 40 nights, was tempted by the devil on three different counts, but he met each attack with the Word. He said, "It is written" each time and then finally proclaimed, "Get behind me Satan, thou shalt serve the Lord thy God and him only shalt thou serve!" She agreed and stated that she was going on a fast. I wanted to say I would fast with her but I knew I had already asked my daughter to get me a steak, potatoes and veggies from Brio's. I also knew that we would probably be going to Georgia on Tuesday or Wednesday for lobster. I also needed to check on my P.O. Box in Florida.

I noticed Victoria was doing the same thing as me: we were writing down different problems that arise as people came up to the counter and complained. My daughter would tell me later the same thing that I encountered: people were angry because we don't offer very much to the lower level players. Even some of the Diamonds and Seven Stars are starting to complain. I believe when we were writing coupons, the guests were happier. I believe the "privilege" was taken away from us because we had quite a number of new staff and there were quite a number of mistakes, because the VIP and/or Sr. Account Executive Hosts wanted to be the ones who wrote the coupons, if need be, and because they wanted the guests to be more responsible and keep up with the coupons. The Marketing and Promotions departments spent hundreds of thousands of dollars printing and mailing these coupons.

Feedback Email and Part II Information

This is the end of Casino Con, Part I – The Ruse. The author invites you to send any questions, comments, or your own experiences to her at: casinoconpart1@gmail.com

Casino Con, Part II – The Revelation is available. Find out how the journey continues.

Book Ordering Information

To order Part II of Casino Con or other books by E.A. James (or books published by FM Publishing Company), or to inquire about screenplay production rights, these distribution points are available:

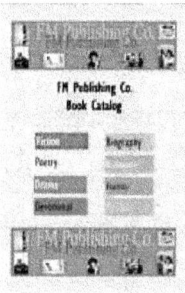

www.fmpublishingcompany.com

www.blackbusinessnetwork.com/doctorlj

www.createspace.com

www.amazon.com

www.ingramSPARKS.com

www.lulu.com

Email: fmpublishing@cox.net

Fax: 800-518-1219

About The Author

Dr. Elizabeth A. James (E.A. James) has been writing for over 40 years. She is a licensed and ordained minister and has been President and Founder of Fast And Indispensable Temporary Help (F.A.I.T.H.) Ministries, Inc. since February, 1999. She is also the Editor-in-Chief of FM Publishing Company (2009) and Senior Managing Director of Geri Lorraine Enterprises, LLC (2000). In 2014, she became a supplier, independent marketer, and supporter with TAG Team Marketing International and a dedicated member of the Black Business Network.

After attending over 10 colleges, she has a doctorate in Theology & Biblical Counseling, a master's in Education, bachelor's degree in English, and major course work in subjects such as Business Management, Biomedical Engineering, Pre-Med, and Chemistry.

In addition to many other accomplishments, E.A. James has received the Woman of Excellence Award, is a member of the blackwritersconnect.com, and has won several awards for her poetry. She is currently a business consultant, certified teacher, and Nationally-Certified Manager of Program Improvement.

Titles by E.A. James:

Spiritual Cosmetics for the Soul (devotionals)
The Last Visitor (historical fiction)
Being a Well Body of Believers (nonfiction)
This Hill I Climb (poetry)
The Reason Why I Sing (poetry/songs)
Driving Tips for BOOHs (Bats Out of Hell) (satire)
7-Day Emergency Help for OWIACs (Of Whom I Am Chief) (devotionals)
Why I Should Hate Men, But Don't (nonfiction)
Will Work for Food, Family & Freedom (nonfiction)
Casino Con: An Eye-Opening Look From the Inside Out (nonfiction)

www.ingramcontent.com/pod-product-compliance
Lightning Source LLC
Chambersburg PA
CBHW071335090426
42738CB00012B/2907